THE CURIOUS WORLD OF DICKENS

The Curious World of

DICKENS

Clive Hurst and Violet Moller

Bodleian Library
UNIVERSITY OF OXFORD

First published in 2012 by the Bodleian Library
Broad Street
Oxford OX1 3BG

www.bodleianbookshop.co.uk

ISBN: 978 1 85124 384 6

Extracts from the following editions of Dickens's novels are reproduced by permission of Oxford University Press:
Barnaby Rudge, Oxford World's Classics, ed. Clive Hurst, Oxford, 2003, 2008
Bleak House, Oxford World's Classics, ed. Stephen Gill, Oxford, 1996, 1998, 2008
A Christmas Carol, Oxford World's Classics, ed. Robert Douglas-Fairhurst, Oxford, 2006, 2008
David Copperfield, Oxford World's Classics, ed. Nina Burgiss and Andrew Sanders, Oxford, 1997, 1999, 2008, 2011
Dombey and Son, Oxford World's Classics, ed. Alan Horsman, Oxford, 1982, 1999, 2001, 2008
The Mystery of Edwin Drood, Oxford World's Classics, ed. Margaret Cardwell, Oxford, 1982, 1999, 2009
Great Expectations, Oxford World's Classics, ed. Margaret Cardwell, Oxford, 1994, 1998, 2008
Martin Chuzzlewit, Oxford World's Classics, ed. Margaret Cardwell, Oxford, 1982, 1984,1998, 2009
Nicholas Nickleby, Oxford World's Classics, ed. Paul Schlicke, Oxford, 1990, 1998, 2008
The Old Curiosity Shop, Oxford World's Classics, ed. E. M. Brennan, Oxford, 1998, 2008
Oliver Twist, Oxford World's Classics, ed. Kathleen Tillotson, Oxford, 1998, 1999, 2008
Our Mutual Friend, Oxford World's Classics, ed. Michael Cotsell, Oxford, 1989, 1998, 2008
The Pickwick Papers, Oxford World's Classics, ed. James Kinsley, Oxford, 1986, 1988, 1998, 2008
A Tale of Two Cities, Oxford World's Classics, ed. Andrew Sanders, Oxford, 1988, 1998, 2008

The extract from Dickens's letter to Miss Burdett Coutts, 16 September 1843 is reproduced by permission of Oxford University Press from the *Pilgrim Edition of the Letters of Charles Dickens*, vol. 3, ed. Graham Storey et al., Oxford, 1974.

The extract from Dickens's letter to W. H. Wills, 3 December 1867 is reproduced by permission of Oxford University Press from the *Pilgrim Edition of the Letters of Charles Dickens*, vol. 11, ed. Graham Storey et al., Oxford, 1999.

Quotation from the *Guardian*, 27 January 2012 reproduced by permission of Guardian News & Media Ltd 2012.

Cover design by Dot Little
Designed and typeset by Dot Little in Bauer Bodoni and Myriad
Printed in Spain on Gardamat 150gr by Grafos SA, Barcelona

British Library Catalogue in Publishing Data
A CIP record of this publication is available from the British Library

CONTENTS

FOREWORD

It is fitting that in the bicentenary of Dickens's birth we should celebrate his novels and the world they inhabit by using some of the Bodleian's collections of ephemera (primarily the John Johnson Collection of Printed Ephemera) and novels in parts. Through playbills, advertisements, murder sheets, maps, panoramas, sheet music, playing cards and prints, we hope to give a flavour of the life and times in which the novels and stories of this great writer were set.

Prompted by quotations from the novels and other works, a selection of the printed material available on the streets of London in the Victorian period is presented here in order to illustrate the matters discussed. So when Mrs Jarley is telling Nell about her travelling waxwork show in *The Old Curiosity Shop*, this is illustrated with a print of a dream at Madame Tussaud's famous exhibition; or when the renowned circus Astley's is visited in the same novel, we have a portrait of the proprietor and prints of the performing horses.

Dickens lived through one of the great innovations of the nineteenth century when the railways transformed Great Britain with a network of speedy connections. When he was a child, his family lived for a while in Camden Town, and he went back to lodge there when his father was in the Marshalsea debtors' prison with his wife and daughter. In *Dombey and Son* he describes the devastating effect of the London & Birmingham line cutting through what was then a village, separated from London by fields and open country, as can be seen on contemporary plans and drawings.

Because of the immediate and huge popularity achieved by his first novel *The Pickwick Papers* in 1836 through to the last, *The Mystery of Edwin Drood*, cruelly interrupted halfway through by the untimely death of the 58-year-old author in 1870, theatres in London and the provinces were keen to get their share of Dickens's success. They commissioned playwrights to adapt the books for the stage, sometimes before the serialization was complete, and the Bodleian has a selection of some of the playbills advertising them. Dickens was a keen thespian himself, and producer of plays, and we can see here from other posters evidence of his activity in this field.

When the Bodleian received by legal deposit copies of the novels in parts, it did what all libraries of the time would do and had them bound, in the process stripping them of their wrappers and advertisements. It was only later that these were recognized as being of academic interest, for literary clues in the wrapper designs (notably the endless speculation over what Dickens told his illustrator about the outcome of *The Mystery of Edwin Drood*), and for the social-historical evidence of the advertisements. The Bodleian has subsequently acquired the original parts, which are what contemporaries saw in their bookshops and stalls appearing on 'Magazine Day' at the end of each month. The experience of reading long novels by instalment, and seeing the illustrations as an integral part of that experience, is something we have largely lost today, but we can have a taste from pictures of the originals.

For permission to reproduce one of the highlights of this book, the earliest surviving letter of Dickens, written to a schoolfellow when he was at the Wellington House Academy, aged thirteen or fourteen, we are most grateful to the Charles Dickens Museum. Thanks are also due to Peter Baldwin of Pollock's Toyshop for the loan of a miniature theatre and permission to reproduce an image of one in these pages, and to Richard Ballam for the loan of a Pope Joan board. The work of conceiving and curating the exhibition has been the responsibility of Clive Hurst, Head of Rare Books at the Bodleian Libraries, and we owe him our thanks as we do Violet Moller for her excellent contribution as co-author of this book.

Sarah E. Thomas
Bodley's Librarian

Introduction

The wide-ranging collection of images in this book illuminates the relationship between the fictional worlds that Charles Dickens created in his novels and the historical reality in which he lived. Of all the great novelists of the nineteenth century no one was more passionately interested in depicting the harsh social realities of that time, particularly in London, than Charles Dickens. More than most writers, he wrote from life, from what he observed all around him—the characters in his novels were often in some way derived from the characters in his life. These extraordinary creations and the powerful scenes in which they operate provide us with the images that, two centuries on, define their age: Oliver asking for more, Pickwick leading the dance, the tragic death of Little Nell, Esther Summerson's humble morality and Dombey's pride and arrogance.

When it comes to illustrating everyday life in the nineteenth century, the John Johnson Collection of Printed Ephemera in the Bodleian Library is an unparalleled resource. Containing over 1.5 million items the collection spans the sixteenth through to the twentieth centuries, but the eighteenth, nineteenth and early twentieth are its strongest areas. Printed ephemera (literally meaning 'short lived') are pieces of textual or illustrative matter that are not intended to last—throwaway items which usually do not survive. Official documents may tell us about the big, important things that happened—governments, wars and so forth—but printed ephemera show us the smaller details: what people wore, what they ate, what they bought and what they did in their spare time. Playbills, posters, handbills, advertisements, prints, scraps, grocers' lists, song sheets, and broadsides—these all reveal the wonder of Dickensian life on the following pages. (Items from the John Johnson Collection are indicated by JJ in the shelfmark).

The themes of this book are wide-ranging and as such reflect not only a broad spectrum of nineteenth-century life, but also the enormous breadth and scope of Charles Dickens's interests. Here was a man who thought

Charles Dickens towards the end of his life, *c.* 1870

Oxford, Bodleian Library, JJ Cartes de Visite 1(5f)

nothing of editing a journal, writing a novel, putting on a play, visiting a prison, giving a dinner party, going to the theatre, walking 15 miles around London, teasing his children and sending a handful of letters—all in a single day. His energy and enthusiasm for life were boundless, and possibly rather exhausting for those around him. The chapters in this book encompass many of these activities: entertainments in London and at home, his professional life, publishing, Christmas books, and the performance side of things. The broader picture is revealed by the sections on railways and London, while Dickens's social reform is examined in chapters on prisons and workhouses, crime and punishment, and education.

For all Dickens's humour and desire to entertain us with his stories, there is a constant current of darkness in his work, which was a true reflection of one of the greatest preoccupations of his life: improving the appalling conditions of the urban working class. He shows us the poor, the dispossessed, the overwhelming cruelty and unfairness of nineteenth-century life. The social reform that drove him in his personal life informs every page of his fiction. They are indivisible from one another, as this extract shows:

> On Thursday night, I went to a Ragged School; and an awful sight it is. I blush to quote Oliver Twist for an authority, but it stands on that ground, and is precisely such a place as the Jew [Fagin] lived in. The school is held in three most wretched rooms on the first floor of a rotten house…
>
> *From a letter to Angela Burdett Coutts, 16 September 1843*

Dickens did not write books merely to entertain; he wrote to educate, to inform and ultimately to change things. In this way his novels complement the work he did in his own time, campaigning for social justice, supporting personal acquaintances financially and emotionally, and working with his close friend, the legendary philanthropist Angela Burdett Coutts. He advised her on the distribution of her enormous charitable donations, and together they set up and ran a home for fallen women in Hammersmith. Dickens has sometimes been accused of sentimentality and a lack of realism, but more often than not the reality he portrayed was simply too tragic and painful for his readers to accept as being possible, let alone probable. As Peter Ackroyd has noted, an example of this is the number of childhood tragedies portrayed in his novels—which have been described as sensationalist and superfluous, but given the fact that in 1839 almost half the funerals in London were for children under the age of ten it would seem that Dickens was simply telling the truth. The unpalatable facts were that the working classes in London had an average mortality age of twenty-two, that the infrastructure of the city was collapsing due to the increasing numbers of immigrants, that there was no proper sanitation system, that the river was a vast open sewer which supplied half the population with water, and that disease, crime, extreme poverty, starvation and squalor were rife.

In spite of Dickens's familiarity with the very worst aspects of the city, he loved it and was entranced by it his whole life. As many critics have observed, London is the biggest character in all of his novels and neither Dickens nor his writing can be separated from it—indeed he was nearly driven mad when trying to write *Dombey* in Switzerland because he missed walking the streets of London so much. Dickens's characters crowd out of the pages with their irrepressible dialogue, strange personal traits and extraordinary energy, just as London comes to life in all of its nineteenth-century filth and glory. The smog, the dirt, the poverty and the multitude of souls squeezed in, cheek by jowl, all scrabbling to survive—here is a city that is at once very familiar and very different. The landmarks and many of the streets are the same, but there are fields on the other side of Regent's Park, Earl's Court is a village and the Thames has not yet been tamed by embankments. One thing that has not changed is the range of diversions on offer. London has ever been a place of amusement, variety and culture, and Dickens was bewitched by the glorious and sometimes murky world of entertainment. Most of all he loved the theatre; whether watching, acting, directing or producing he was fascinated by it and explored it joyfully in his fiction.

Dickensian London was a city split into two: those who had good jobs, nice houses, warm hearths and food on the table—and the rest. If Dickens had one mission in his life it was to make the first group look at what was happening to the second group, care about it, and do something to help. This one theme underlay his writing and his philanthropy. Given the peculiarities of his own childhood it is not surprising that the fate and condition of children was such an important part of his work. Many of his most memorable characters are children, and a significant proportion of his social campaigning was concerned with schooling and the care of the young, particularly in institutions. The concept of childhood as we know it today began during the nineteenth century. This included the conviction that children were not merely small adults, but that they had their own particular set of needs in order to develop properly. The importance of playing, of simply being allowed to enjoy being a child rather than being trained to be an adult or being put to work, was fundamental to this, as was the development of literature written specifically for the young that also flourished in the nineteenth century. These ideals were easy to apply to wealthy children, but it was a different matter for the working classes and the dispossessed. Dickens recognised all this. In *The Old Curiosity Shop*, he has Little Nell's grandfather

Charles Dickens seated in his study, *c.* **1870**

Oxford, Bodleian Library, JJ Cartes de Visite 1(5d)

say, 'Besides, the children of the poor know but few pleasures. Even the cheap delights of childhood must be bought and paid for' (Chapter 1).

The nineteenth century was a time of great social change, mainly for the better, but progress was often slow. Improvements in education ensured that literacy rates increased steadily. This created new readerships, which in turn affected the publishing industry. Many more readers could afford the monthly cost of a shilling to buy the next instalment of a novel—where a whole book would have been too expensive. *The Pickwick Papers* was the first serialised novel in Britain to become really successful and it established a pattern not only for the rest of Dickens's novels, but also for how fiction was written and published. Literature was being democratised and Dickens was leading the charge. Serial publication also increased sales by creating an atmosphere of common suspense, similar to the effect of a television soap opera today. Large numbers of people were reading the stories, talking about them and then waiting with bated breath for the next instalment; so much so that in America crowds of people waited on the quayside for the ship carrying the latest instalment to see whether Little Nell had died or not. It soon became a popular way to publish fiction and others followed suit, including Dickens's friend Wilkie Collins (author of *The Moonstone* and father of the modern detective novel), Anthony Trollope and Thackeray. In Russia, Tolstoy serialised *Anna Karenina* and in France Flaubert's *Madame Bovary* was also published this way.

Another innovation was the inclusion of illustrations with each part. Dickens worked with many different artists over the years, and the pictures they produced have become almost as iconic as the novels themselves. They are still used today as major points of reference for anyone adapting a book for film, television or the stage. Dickens's longest-standing and most important collaborator was Hablot Browne—better known as Phiz (the pseudonym he took to go with Dickens's Boz). His best-known work is in

The Pickwick Papers, Nicholas Nickleby, Dombey and Son, David Copperfield, Bleak House and *Little Dorrit*. His style was comic and irreverent, and he and Dickens worked closely together for twenty-three years. Dickens made the facial expressions himself for his characters—leaping up and checking in the mirror that they looked right.

The coming of the railways in the early part of the century was another great step into the future. Dickens watched the progress of the London & Birmingham railway as it tore through the neighbourhoods of Camden and Somers Town, where he had lived as a boy. He saw the destruction that was wrought on both the environment and the population—who were often forced out of their homes without being rehoused, further adding to the desperate housing problems in the capital. Dickens examined the wider theme of the damage caused by industrialisation (with the railways being an integral part of this process) in his novel *Dombey and Son*, written between 1846 and 1848—one of the busiest decades in railway construction.

For someone who lived so intensely and publicly, Dickens was also remarkably fond of his family and his home. The Dickenses moved numerous times but initially theirs seems to have been a happy existence; filled with extravagant dinners for friends, ambitious theatricals, merry Christmases, children's parties and a lot more fun than would normally be associated with a Victorian home. Dickens was always at the centre: orchestrating, entertaining and controlling everyone in his vortex of mad energy. Like many great men, however, he was by many accounts also deeply flawed: selfish, moody and at times completely irrational. In 1858 the happy home fell apart dramatically when he left his long-suffering wife, Catherine. She had borne him ten children, been a dutiful wife, and even written a book on how to run a successful kitchen. It is ironic that his eventual treatment of her cast him in the same role as some of the more detestable creations in his books.

Through his boundless energy and intelligence, Charles Dickens lived a truly extraordinary life, encompassing in his interests and his experiences a vast range of people, places, ideas and events. His writing naturally reflected this, and created for us a world that is at once enchanting and horrifying, joyful and sad, comic and tragic. The wide variety of images in this book illustrate this, providing a window on both of Charles Dickens's worlds—the real one he inhabited, and the one inside his head.

1 DICKENS AND EDUCATION

Schools in Victorian England varied enormously because there was no real standardisation of education. Anyone could open a school (as Dickens's mother did—unsuccessfully—in 1823) and as a result some children received a good education from kind, sympathetic adults while others at the other end of the spectrum endured shocking cruelty and little effective teaching. Charles Dickens's own education was patchy at best. His mother taught him to read as a child and he enjoyed reading stories—there is a lot of the young Charles in the description of David Copperfield loving the store of books left to him by his father. He enjoyed Mr Giles's school in Chatham, but when financial problems forced the family to move to London, Charles was sent to work in a blacking factory instead of to another school. This period of his life marked him like no other; it had a huge influence over his views on childhood, child labour and the importance of education. He was never able to forget, or to understand why his parents treated him in this way. He did, however, eventually attend a school—Wellington House—in London, which he enjoyed more for the games, camaraderie and return to childhood than for its academic excellence, and which was one of the inspirations for Salem House in *David Copperfield*. He seems to have managed to avoid the notoriously vicious headmaster there, but did later research the famously brutal Yorkshire schools and exposed them in *Nicholas Nickleby*. These formative experiences were important elements in Dickens's interest in schools and belief in the transformative power of a good education, just as they informed the child characters and descriptions of schooling in his novels.

MY FATHER had left in a little room up-stairs, to which I had access (for it adjoined my own) a small collection of books which nobody else in our house ever troubled. From that blessed little room, Roderick Random, Peregrine Pickle, Humphrey Clinker, Tom Jones, The Vicar of Wakefield, Don Quixote, Gil Blas, and Robinson Crusoe, came out, a glorious host, to keep me company. They kept alive my fancy, and my hope of something beyond that place and time,—they, and the Arabian Nights, and the Tales of the Genii,—and did me no harm; for whatever harm was in some of them was not there for me; *I* knew nothing of it. It is astonishing to me now, how I found time, in the midst of my porings and blunderings over heavier themes, to read those books as I did.

David Copperfield, **Chapter 4.**

Silhouette of Dickens with mortarboard, 1826
Extracted from *The Connoisseur*, 28, December 1910.

This portrait was taken when Dickens was about fourteen years old, and attending Wellington House Academy. He left school for good the following year, just after his fifteenth birthday.

Oxford, Bodleian Library, JJ Dickens 1(2)

Letter to O.P. Thomas, *c.* 1825–6 (above)

A Greek and English Lexicon, 1825, and
Clavis Virgiliana, 1815 (left)

A letter from schoolboy Charles Dickens to his friend Tom, thought to be written when Dickens was thirteen or fourteen:

'Tom, I am quite ashamed I have not returned your Leg but you shall have it by Harry to morrow. If you would like to purchase my Clavis you shall have it at a *very reduced price*. Cheaper in comparison than a Leg. Yours &c C Dickens PS I suppose all this time you have had a *wooden* leg. I have weighed yours every saturday Night.'

'Leg' here is short for *Lexicon*, which is an Ancient Greek dictionary, and the *Clavis* is a vocabulary of the works of Virgil. Both would have been school reference books. This is the earliest surviving letter by Dickens.

Letter reproduced courtesy of The Charles Dickens Museum, London.
Oxford, Bodleian Library, Lexicon: 25.588; Clavis: 305 e.43

SHADOW versus SUBSTANCE.

LORD B—— laid a bet on two game-cocks, that they,
When pitted, would turn from each other away;
So, next day, in Boots of resplendence grand,
By WARREN'S famed Jet, No. 30, the Strand,
He came when relinquishing grosser pursuits,
The cocks fiercely flew at the mirror-like Boots,
And each on his shadow made desp'rate attack,
Nor could they again to the scratch be brought back;
Thus triumph'd Lord B——, WARREN'S Blacking the cause
Of vict'ry, while hail'd with unbounded applause.

This Easy-shining and brilliant Blacking, prepared by RO-
BERT WARREN, 30, Strand, London; and sold in every town
in the kingdom. Liquid, in Bottles, and Paste Blacking, in
Pots, at 6d., 12d., and 18d. each.
Be particular to enquire for WARREN'S, 30, Strand.
All others are counterfeit.

Warren's Blacking advertisements, 1852

These advertisements were for blacking, or shoe polish, similar to that which Charles Dickens worked with. His job at Warren's factory was sticking labels on the pots of blacking. On describing his work at Murdstone and Grinby's warehouse David Copperfield writes: 'No words can express the secret agony of my soul as I sunk into this companionship; compared these henceforth everyday associates with those of my happier childhood … and felt my hopes of growing up to be a learned and distinguished man, crushed in my bosom' (Chapter 11). This is one of Dickens's most autobiographical pieces of writing.

Oxford, Bodleian Library, JJ Oil and Candles 1 (29c) and (30)

THE TRIUMPH OF MERIT.

When first from the Mart, Number 30, the Strand,
The Jet emanated, to polish each land,
There sprung up of impotent rivals a host;
But where are they now? In obscurity lost!
The Blacking of WARREN, while spreading its name,
And gaining distinguished and permanent fame,
Through intrinsic worth, for its splendour unfurl'd,
Pervades now the whole of the civiliz'd world!

This easy-shining and brilliant Blacking, prepared by

Robert Warren

30, Strand, London; and sold in every town in the kingdom. Liquid, in Bottles, and
Paste Blacking, in Pots, at 6d., 12d. and 18d. each.—☞ Be particular to inquire for
Warren's, 30, Strand.—All others are counterfeit.

The School Regulator; or Semi-annual Register of the Study and Conduct of Young Gentlemen, by William Bransby Faiers. London, 1823.

The half-yearly report for a Master Frost at a similar school to Dickens's, showing the variety of subjects taught at these schools, the concern for conduct, and the manner of marking. Frost was obviously a pretty average scholar, getting nearly all Bs. The marks could range from 'Quam optime' (excellent) to 'Quam pessime' (extremely poor); B or Bene was satisfactory. This particular school seems, unusually, not to have taught languages.

Oxford, Bodleian Library, JJ Educational 4, centrefold, with marks enhanced

Bill for Master Montgomery's schooling, Christmas 1823 to Midsummer 1824

A half-yearly bill for another school similar to the Wellington Academy. It shows all the things Montgomery's father or guardian had to pay for in addition to general board and instruction, including special tuition, such as military exercise, and living expenses including clothes, laundry, haircuts and books. Dotheboys' Hall offered a similar curriculum in Squeers's prospectus, but in reality gave only ignorance and suffering.

Oxford, Bodleian Library, JJ Educational 9

ARE YOU WILLING to work, sir?' he inquired, frowning on his nephew.

'Of course I am,' replied Nicholas haughtily.

'Then see here, sir,' said his uncle. 'This caught my eye this morning, and you may thank your stars for it.'

With this exordium, Mr. Ralph Nickleby took a newspaper from his pocket, and after unfolding it, and looking for a short time among the advertisements, read as follows:

"'EDUCATION.—At Mr. Wackford Squeers's Academy, Dotheboys Hall, at the delightful village of Dotheboys, near Greta Bridge in Yorkshire, Youth are boarded, clothed, booked, furnished with pocket-money, provided with all necessaries, instructed in all languages living and dead, mathematics, orthography, geometry, astronomy, trigonometry, the use of the globes, algebra, single stick (if required), writing, arithmetic, fortification, and every other branch of classical literature. Terms, twenty guineas per annum. No extras, no vacations, and diet unparalleled. Mr. Squeers is in town, and attends daily, from one till four, at the Saracen's Head, Snow Hill. N.B. An able assistant wanted. Annual salary £5. A Master of Arts would be preferred."'

'There!' said Ralph, folding the paper again. 'Let him get that situation, and his fortune is made.'

'But he is not a Master of Arts,' said Mrs. Nickleby.

'That,' replied Ralph, 'that, I think, can be got over.'

Nicholas Nickleby, **Chapter 3**

'A School in Uproar', *c.* 1840, monochrome print

David Copperfield describes a Saturday afternoon at Salem House boarding school: 'If I could associate the idea of a bull or a bear with any one so mild as Mr. Mell, I should think of him, in connexion with that afternoon when the uproar was at its height, as one of those animals, baited by ten thousand dogs. I recall him bending his aching head … and wretchedly endeavouring to get on with his tiresome work, amidst an uproar that might have made the Speaker of the House of Commons giddy. Boys started in and out of their places, playing at Puss in the Corner with other boys; there were laughing boys, singing boys, talking boys, dancing boys, howling boys; boys shuffled with their feet…' (Chapter 7).

Oxford, Bodleian Library, JJ Educational 14

 **LONDON**

London is the setting for almost all of Charles Dickens's novels. Although born in Portsmouth, he lived in London on and off all his life, but his first real experiences of the city came in the early 1820s when the family moved from Chatham. His parents' debt crisis meant that Charles, at the age of eleven, was sent to work in a blacking factory, sticking labels onto pots. He also spent time living apart from his family—who were by now in the Marshalsea debtors' prison. This was an extremely hard period in Dickens's life, but it was also when he first fell in love with London: the mighty landmarks, the stinking, crowded river, the swirling smog and most of all the multitude of extraordinary characters who would come to inspire and populate his stories. At this time he also began his lifelong habit of walking around the city observing and thinking as he went. Sometimes this was out of necessity—he had to walk to work at the factory each day—but it soon became part of the fabric of his life and later was a vital part of his writing process. There are many links between Dickens's real life in London and the London he created in his pages, and none is stronger than those in the semi-autobiographical *David Copperfield*. Skimpole in *Bleak House* lives in The Polygon, where Dickens himself lived for a while, and there was an orphan boy called Bob Fagin working in the blacking factory. On a more profound level, it was the shocking contrast between 'wealth and poverty' and their proximity to one another in London that Dickens described so accurately in his novels—as in *Nicholas Nickleby*, where 'repletion and starvation laid them down together'.

THEY RATTLED ON through the noisy, bustling, crowded streets of London, now displaying long double rows of brightly-burning lamps, dotted here and there with the chemists' glaring lights, and illuminated besides with the brilliant flood that streamed from the windows of the shops, where sparkling jewellery, silks and velvets of the richest colours, the most inviting delicacies, and most sumptuous articles of luxurious ornament, succeeded each other in rich and glittering profusion. Streams of people apparently without end poured on and on, jostling each other in the crowd and hurrying forward, scarcely seeming to notice the riches that surrounded them on every side; while vehicles of all shapes and makes, mingled up together in one moving mass like running water, lent their ceaseless roar to swell the noise and tumult.

As they dashed by the quickly-changing and ever-varying objects, it was curious to observe in what a strange procession they passed before the eye. Emporiums of splendid dresses, the materials brought from every quarter of the world; tempting stores of everything to stimulate and pamper the sated appetite and give new relish to the oft-repeated feast; vessels of burnished gold and silver, wrought into every exquisite form of vase, and dish, and goblet; guns, swords, pistols, and patent engines of destruction; screws and irons for the crooked, clothes for the newly-born, drugs for the sick, coffins for the dead, churchyards for the buried—all these jumbled each with the other and flocking side by side, seemed to flit by in motley dance like the fantastic groups of the old Dutch painter, and with the same stern moral for the unheeding restless crowd.

Nor were there wanting objects in the crowd itself to give new point and purpose to the shifting scene. The rags of the squalid ballad-singer fluttered in the rich light that showed the goldsmith's treasures; pale and pinched-up faces hovered about the windows where was tempting food; hungry eyes wandered over the profusion guarded by one thin sheet of brittle glass— an iron wall to them; half-naked shivering figures stopped to gaze at Chinese shawls and golden stuffs of India. There was a christening party at the largest coffin-maker's and a funeral hatchment had stopped some great improvements in the bravest mansion. Life and death went hand in hand; wealth and poverty stood side by side; repletion and starvation laid them down together.

Nicholas Nickleby, **Chapter 32.**

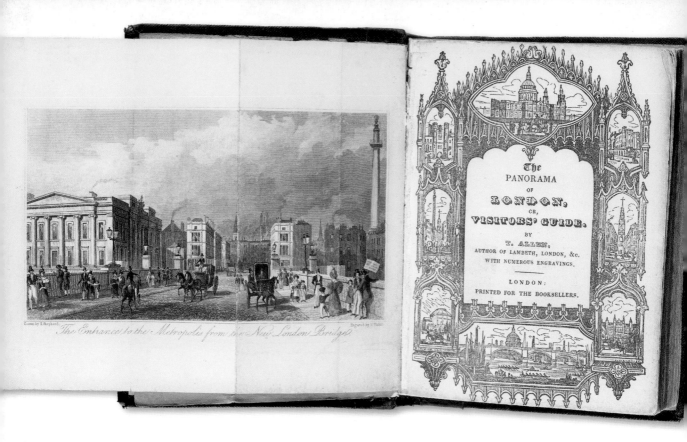

The Panorama of London, or, Visitors' Guide, 1837

Title page and frontispiece showing carriages on the New London Bridge, the entrance to the metropolis from the south over the river. As such it provides a first view of London proper, similar to that which Nicholas Nickleby would have seen on his journey into the city.

Oxford, Bodleian Library, Vet. A6 f. 1023

New Plan of London, 1839

Reversed out map of London.

Doughty Street, where Charles Dickens and his wife had their first proper family home at no. 48, is named on this map. They lived there from 1837 to 1839.

Oxford, Bodleian Library, Vet. A6 f. 1023

NEW PLAN OF
LONDON
1839.

Published for the Proprietors of the Guide to London

SCALE OF HALF A MILE

Detail from *The Grand Panorama of London from the Thames*, presented to subscribers to the *Pictorial Times*, 1844

This panorama was published a year after a very similar one was presented to subscribers of *The Illustrated London News*. The image shows how wide the river was before the embankments were built, and how incredibly crowded it was—full of boats of all sizes, and still with a claim to being 'London's busiest thoroughfare'. The dilapidated Hungerford Bridge is in the middle of the picture; the old Hungerford Stairs would have been at the far end of it. As Dickens remembers in the autobiographical fragment published by John Forster, this was where he worked for a time: 'The blacking warehouse was the last house on the left-hand side of the way, at old Hungerford Stairs. It was a crazy, tumbledown old house, abutting of course on the river, and literally overrun with rats.'

Oxford, Bodleian Library, G.A. Lond. 16°193

RICHARD SWIVELLER took a greasy memorandum-book from his pocket and made an entry therein.

'Is that a reminder, in case you should forget to call?' said Trent with a sneer.

'Not exactly, Fred,' replied the imperturbable Richard, continuing to write with a business-like air, 'I enter in this little book the names of the streets that I can't go down while the shops are open. This dinner to-day closes Long Acre. I bought a pair of boots in Great Queen Street last week, and made that no thoroughfare too. There's only one avenue to the Strand left open now, and I shall have to stop up that to-night with a pair of gloves. The roads are closing so fast in every direction, that in about a month's time, unless my aunt sends me a remittance, I shall have to go three or four miles out of town to get over the way.'

The Old Curiosity Shop, **Chapter 8.**

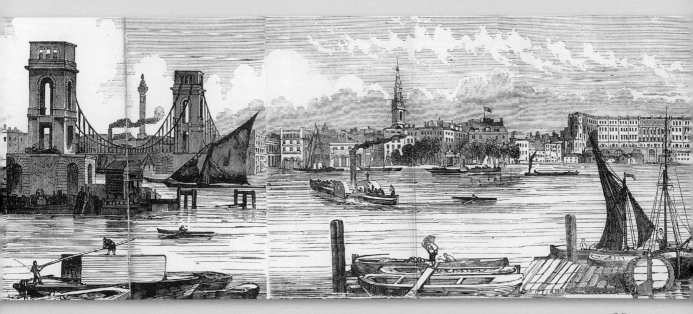

27   29   31   33   35   Richard Read,   37   PICCADILLY.   39   Loyd & Co.'s Cigar Divan,   41   43   Samuel Nock,   45   5
                                      Surgical Instrument Maker.   REGENT   CIRCUS.   17 Tichbourne Street.   Gun-maker to the Queen.

Grand Architectural Panorama of London, 1849

Sections showing Regent Street and Piccadilly.

In *David Copperfield*, Mr Micawber talks about his desire to move out of Camden Town: 'There would probably be an interval, he explained, in which he should content himself with the upper part of a house, over some respectable place of business,—say in Piccadilly,—which would be a cheerful situation for Mrs. Micawber; and where, by throwing out a bow-window, or carrying up the roof another story, or making some little alteration of that sort, they might live, comfortably and reputably, for a few years' (Chapter 28).

Oxford, Bodleian Library, G.A. Lond. 16° 187

47　49　51　60 Opposite. L. Barbe,　53　55　57　68 Opposite. R. Rendall,　59　61　62 Opposite. W. Allcroft,　63　VINE STREET.　65. J. Field,　67　69
Artist Colorman.　Chiropodist.　Stationer and Opera Agent.　Agent for Morrison's Pills.

Tallis's London Street Views c. 1840

The Nicklebys have lodgings on the Strand and
Miss La Creevy, their portrait artist landlady,
remarks: 'To carry out an idea … that's the
great convenience of living in a thoroughfare
like the Strand. When I want a nose or an eye
for any particular sitter, I have only to look out
of window and wait till I get one' (Chapter 5).

Oxford, Bodleian Library, Don. d. 101, no. 19

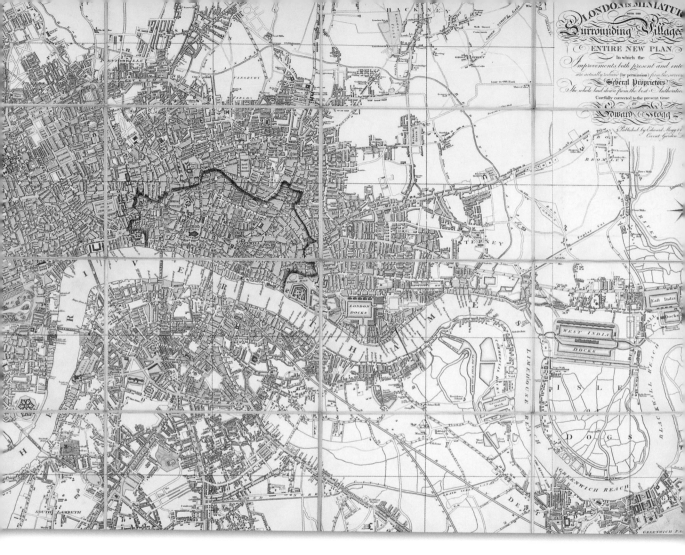

London in miniature, 1839

A miniature map of London and surrounding villages.

This map clearly shows the development of London at this time. Primrose Hill is in the countryside, Camden Town is partially built, right on the edge of the city, and the 'surrounding villages' include Earls Court, Bethnal Green and Hackney.

Oxford, Bodleian Library, (E) c17:70 London (634)

THE DIVERSIONS
OF LONDON

Dickens's London was awash with theatres, sights, playhouses, museums, parks and amphitheatres that offered a huge range of entertainment. Wonders and marvels, freak shows, plays, world-famous performers, terrifying animals, feats of extraordinary daring and strength—these were all on display to those who could afford a ticket. This was a golden age of entertainment when Philip Astley invented the circus as we know it, Madame Tussaud established a permanent exhibition of waxworks in Baker Street, and the legendary Joseph Grimaldi created the modern-day clown. Charles Dickens was introduced to this magical world as a child when he was taken to London to see Grimaldi in pantomime. This marked the beginning of Dickens's lifelong love affair with the stage, and this passion is reflected by the many examples of London performers and entertainments that feature in his novels, and in his editing of Grimaldi's *Memoirs* in 1838. He included a visit to Astley's in *The Old Curiosity Shop*, and in the same novel he reinvented Madame Tussaud, the doyenne of waxworks, as Mrs Jarley. Nineteenth-century entertainment was generally intended to make audiences laugh, or gasp in wonder, but, as Mrs Jarley points out, some things were meant to be different—'calm and classical' like her waxworks or dark and downright creepy like the so-called human freaks.

DEAR, DEAR, what a place it looked, that Astley's! with all the paint, gilding, and looking-glass, the vague smell of horses suggestive of coming wonders, the curtain that hid such gorgeous mysteries, the clean white sawdust down in the circus, the company coming in and taking their places; the fiddlers looking carelessly up at them while they tuned their instruments, as if they didn't want the play to begin, and knew it all beforehand! What a glow was that which burst upon them all, when that long, clear, brilliant row of lights came slowly up; and what the feverish excitement when the little bell rang and the music began in good earnest, with strong parts for the drums, and sweet effects for the triangles!…

Then the play itself! the horses which little Jacob believed from the first to be alive, and the ladies and gentlemen of whose reality he could be by no means persuaded, having never seen or heard anything at all like them—the firing, which made Barbara wink—the forlorn lady, who made her cry—the tyrant, who made her tremble—the man who sung the song with the lady's-maid and danced the chorus, who made her laugh—the pony who reared up on his hind legs when he saw the murderer, and wouldn't hear of walking on all fours again until he was taken into custody—the clown who ventured on such familiarities with the military man in boots—the lady who jumped over the nine-and-twenty ribbons and came down safe upon the horse's back—everything was delightful, splendid, and surprising.

The Old Curiosity Shop, **Chapter 39**.

Astley's ROYAL GROVE & AMPHITHEATRE RIDING HOUSE,
Westminster Bridge.

Prints of Astley's Royal Grove & Amphitheatre Riding House, Westminster Bridge, *c.* 1790 and A Circus Interior, *c.* 1830

In *The Old Curiosity Shop*, Kit and Barbara take their mothers on a trip to Astley's Theatre: 'Well might Barbara's mother say to Kit's mother that the gallery was the place to see from, and wonder it wasn't much dearer than the boxes; and well might Barbara feel doubtful whether to laugh or cry, in her flutter of delight' (Chapter 39).

Oxford, Bodleian Library, JJ Circuses 1 (4) and JJ Circuses 3 (41)

Watercolour portrait of Philip Astley, *c.* 1810

Astley is credited with devising the modern circus. In 1846 Queen Victoria and Prince Albert, together with the Prince of Wales and the Princess Royal, visited Astley's Royal Amphitheatre. The *Pictorial Times* reported that the prince and princess 'appeared to be completely amazed at the brilliant *tout ensemble*'.

Oxford, Bodleian Library, JJ Circuses 1 (4)

Mr. Ducrow's 'feats of horsemanship' (at Astley's Theatre), *c.* 1820

An early example of Fairburn's scraps. Scraps were illustrations and drawings sold in sheets for children to cut up and stick into albums, hence 'scrapbooks'. Ducrow is mentioned in *Sketches by Boz* and in *Bleak House:* Mr. George 'stops hard by Waterloo Bridge, and reads a playbill; decides to go to Astley's Theatre. Being there, is much delighted with the horses and the feats of strength' (Chapter 21).

Oxford, Bodleian Library, JJ Circuses 1 (8)

A feat of horsemanship, *c.* 1820

Fairburn's scraps. Trick riders such as these could have provided the inspiration for Mr Sleary and his equestrian circus act in *Hard Times*.

Oxford, Bodleian Library, JJ Circuses 4 (11a)

Grimaldi as clown in *Mother Goose*, 1846

Aquatint of a portrait by Samuel de Wilde. Grimaldi the clown makes an appearance as one of Mrs Jarley's waxworks in *The Old Curiosity Shop*.

Oxford, Bodleian Library, JJ Circuses 3 (53)

Portrait of Joseph Grimaldi, *c.* 1820

Mezzotint after the portrait by John Cawse.

Oxford, Bodleian Library, JJ Circuses 3 (54)

'The female Blondin. As she appeared crossing the Thames on a tight rope from Cremorne Gardens', 1861

Hand-coloured print. Charles Blondin was a renowned tight-rope walker who achieved fame for crossing the gorge below Niagara Falls. He inspired both men and women to attempt similar feats. When Dickens witnessed one of his performances, he thought that half the audience was there waiting for an accident.

Oxford, Bodleian Library, JJ Circuses 4 (59)

NELL WALKED DOWN IT, and read aloud, in enormous black letters, the inscription, 'Jarley's WAX-WORK.'

'Read it again,' said the lady, complacently.

'Jarley's Wax-Work,' repeated Nell.

'That's me,' said the lady. 'I am Mrs. Jarley.'

Giving the child an encouraging look, intended to reassure her and let her know, that, although she stood in the presence of the original Jarley, she must not allow herself to be utterly overwhelmed and borne down, the lady of the caravan unfolded another scroll, whereon was the inscription, 'One hundred figures the full size of life', and then another scroll, on which was written, 'The only stupendous collection of real wax-work in the world', and then several smaller scrolls with such inscriptions as 'Now exhibiting within'—'The genuine and only Jarley'—'Jarley's unrivalled collection'—'Jarley is the delight of the Nobility and Gentry'—'The Royal Family are the patrons of Jarley'. ...

'I never saw any wax-work, ma'am,' said Nell. 'Is it funnier than Punch?'

'Funnier!' said Mrs. Jarley in a shrill voice. 'It is not funny at all.'

'Oh!' said Nell, with all possible humility.

'It isn't funny at all,' repeated Mrs. Jarley. 'It's calm and—what's that word again—critical?—no—classical, that's it—it's calm and classical. No low beatings and knockings about, no jokings and squeakings like your precious Punches, but always the same, with a constantly unchanging air of coldness and gentility; and so like life, that if wax-work only spoke and walked about, you'd hardly know the difference. I won't go so far as to say, that, as it is, I've seen wax-work quite like life, but I've certainly seen some life that was exactly like wax-work.'

The Old Curiosity Shop, **Chapter 27**

Portrait print of Madame Tussaud, *c.* 1840

Dickens modelled Mrs Jarley on Marie Tussaud, who established a permanent exhibition of waxworks in Baker Street, which later moved to Marylebone Road. An estimated 500 million people have visited what is now known as Madame Tussaud's since it was first established.

Oxford, Bodleian Library, JJ Waxworks 2 (34b)

Madame Tussaud's exhibition, Bazaar, Baker Street, *c.* 1835–44

Print of an interior scene from Madame Tussaud's first permanent exhibition, based at Baker Street. Illustration by Henry Melville.

Oxford, Bodleian Library, JJ Waxworks 2 (34a)

'I dreamt I slept at Madame Tussaud's', *c.* 1847

Cartoon by George Cruikshank.

Print of a fantastical cartoon by George Cruikshank, in which Napoleon waltzes with Mme Tussaud, Britannia bows her shield with her trident, and Henry VIII looks on, smoking a pipe.

Oxford, Bodleian Library, JJ Waxworks 2 (33)

Poster for the Royal Gallery of Wax Models, the Cheapside Tragedy, *c.* 1840

An example of the kind of macabre subject matter popular with the creators of waxwork exhibitions.

Oxford, Bodleian Library, JJ Waxworks 3 (7)

FOR A SHORT TIME ONLY.

AT THE LARGE ROOM, FOX INN,
BILSTON.

ROYAL GALLERY
OF WAX
MODELS,
THE
CHEAPSIDE
TRAGEDY.

The Public are respectfully informed, that the Proprietor of the above popular Exhibition has just added to the Collection a faithful representation of the late

Horrible Murders

perpetrated on Four innocent Children by their own

MOTHER,

The whole Copied from Drawings taken the Morning of the Discovery.

The Room in which the Group is exhibited has been made an exact *fac-simile* of the

Fatal Chamber in which the Bloody Deed was done, and represents the whole scene as it appeared the moment the entrance was made by Mr. Edwards.

Ladies and Gentlemen who object to such sights are respectfully informed that this Group is fitted up in a separate Room, and will only be shown to such persons as desire it.

REMEMBER! AT THE FOX INN.

Admission---2d.   Children Half Price.

FOR PARTICULARS SEE LARGE BILLS.

Poster for 'Dr. Kahn's Anatomical Museum', 1853

This exhibition took place at the Portland Gallery in Regent Street and featured wax models showing 'the anatomy of muscles, arteries, veins, and nerves', 'the famous Caesarean Operation' and 'extraordinary freaks of nature'. In *Nicholas Nickleby*, Wackford Squeers talks of 'cadaverous old Slider … who I wish was dead and buried, and resurrected and dissected, and hung upon wires in a anatomical museum, before ever I'd had anything to do with her' (Chapter 60).

Oxford, Bodleian Library, JJ Waxworks 3 (26)

Poster for 'The Parisian Venus', c. 1820–50

Advertisement for an exhibition of female anatomy in waxwork.

Oxford, Bodleian Library, JJ Waxworks 3 (34)

The Saturday Magazine, The Monument, 1833

Issue of *The Saturday Magazine*, 23 March 1833, showing a 'View of the new opening to the Monument of London'. In *Barnaby Rudge*, John Willet advises his son Joe about what to do in the capital: '[T]he diversion I recommend is going to the top of the Monument, and sitting there. There's no temptation there, sir—no drink—no young women—no bad characters of any sort—nothing but imagination. That's the way I enjoyed myself when I was your age, sir' (Chapter 13).

Oxford, Bodleian Library, London Play Places 4(28)

Mansell's Guide to the Amusements of London for 1847

This single-sheet guide to the plethora of entertainments available in Dickens's London lists Madame Tussaud's Baker Street Bazaar—'public characters, living and dead, modelled in wax with great skill, dressed in appropriate costume'—and The Monument—'Visitors are allowed to ascend by stairs to the top by paying 6d. each'—among many other attractions.

Oxford, Bodleian Library, JJ Entertainments folder 11 (24)

Saturday Magazine.

Nᵒ 46.   MARCH   23ᴿᴰ, 1833.   { PRICE ONE PENNY

UNDER THE DIRECTION OF THE COMMITTEE OF GENERAL LITERATURE AND EDUCATION, APPOINTED BY THE SOCIETY FOR PROMOTING CHRISTIAN KNOWLEDGE.

MANSELL'S
GUIDE TO THE AMUSEMENTS OF LONDON
For 1847.

PRICE ONE PENNY.

...IC BUILDINGS.	Time of Admission and Price.	REMARKS.	BRIDGES.
...er of London, Bottom ... Thames-street, in which Street ...agate, the most celebrated ...for Fish in the world, also the ...a House, the long room of ...will repay the visitor for a	Daily, 10 to 4. 1s. The Wardens of the Tower are in attendance from 10 to 4, to conduct visitors at the following charges :— To the Armories ....6d. To the Jewel Office ....6d.	The Tower of London, which forms one of the principal sights of the metropolis, is a cluster of houses, towers, and prison-like edifices, situated in a low and obscure locality, on the north bank of the Thames and separated from the crowded narrow streets of the city by an open space of ground called Tower-hill. The Tower was founded by William the Conqueror, to secure his authority over the inhabitants of London ; but the original fort which he established on the spot was greatly extended by subsequent monarchs ; and in the twelfth century it was surrounded by a wet ditch, which was greatly improved during the reign of Charles II. Within the outer wall the ground measures upwards of twelve acres. Next the river there is a broad quay, and on this side also there is a channel by which boats may pass into the main body of the place. This water entrance is known by the name of Traitor's Gate, being that by which state prisoners are conveyed out to boats to proceed for trial at Westminster. The interior of the Tower is an irregular assemblage of short streets and court-yards, with barracks, houses of keepers, &c. The chief buildings are—the White Tower for prisoners, an ancient chapel, the Ordnance-Office, the Record-Office, the Jewel-Office, the Horse Armoury, the Grand Storehouse, and the Small Armoury. Strangers, on applying at an office at the entrance from Tower-hill, are conducted through the public establishments. The principal objects of curiosity are the immense store of fire-arms, sufficient to equip upwards of 150,000 men ; a collection of cannon, being trophies of war ; the horse armoury, being a most interesting collection of suits of mail, on figures ; and the jewel office, the crown and other insignia of royalty.	London Bridge is situate at the eastern extremity of Lombard and King William street, and divides the City from the Borough of Southwark. The site of it is about 100 feet west-ward of the old Bridge, which stood in a direct line from Gracechurch-street and Fish-street Hill : the first pile was driven in 1824, and the first stone on the Surrey side was laid in June, 1825 ; the first stone on the City side was laid August 1, 1827. It was opened by William IV. on the 1st August, 1831. The bridge consists of five very beautiful elliptical arches, the two outwardmost of which are 130 feet in span, and 27½ feet in height, being the largest elliptical stone in existence.
...s Cathedral, St. Paul's ...yard, top of Ludgate-hill, and ...an account of its high position ...an excellent landmark for all ...e the Metropolis, as is can be ...seen for miles round the me-	Daily, 10 till dusk. 4s. 4d. The Vergers are in attendance, and the following are the charges to the Metropolitan Cathedral :— To the Monuments to England's heroes ....0 2 Galleries ....0 6 Vaults 0 0	St. Paul's Cathedral, from its vast dimensions, great height, and commanding position, on an eminence north of the Thames, may be regarded as the most conspicuous edifice in the metropolis, while its architectural merits render it one of the most magnificent. The ancient Gothic cathedral, which originally stood on the same spot, was destroyed in the great fire of London, A.D. 1666 ; and the erection of the present building was intrusted to Sir Christopher Wren, under whose direction the first stone was laid in 1675. The highest or last stone on the top of the lantern was laid by Mr. Christopher Wren, the son of the great architect, in the year 1710 ; and thus was this noble fabric, lofty enough to be discerned at sea eastward, and at Windsor to the West, begun and completed in the space of thirty-five years by one architect, that one Sir Christopher Wren ; one principal mason, Mr. Strong ; and under one Bishop of London, Dr. Henry Compton ; whereas St. Peter's at Rome, the only structure that can come in competition with it, continued 155 years in building, under twelve successive architects, assisted by the police and interests of the Roman see. The principal entrance or front, which looks westward, is adorned with a rich and beautiful portico, consisting of twelve lofty Corinthian pillars below, and above are eight composite ones, ranged in pairs, supporting a triangular pediment, the entablature of which represents the conversion of St. Paul, sculptured by Bird in low relief. On the apex of the pediment is a colossal figure of St. Paul, with two of equal size at each end, representing St. Peter and St. James ; and along the summit of the front are similar statues of the four Evangelists. The angels are surrounded by bell towers, of a chaste and uniform cha-...	Waterloo Bridge was begun in 1811, and opened on 18th June, 1817. The bridge, approaches, &c. cost a sum considerably above £1,000,000, besides a loan from Government of £60,000 on Mortgage of the tolls. The bridge consists of nine arches, each of 120 feet span, the piers are 20 feet thick, and each stands upon a platform based on 320 piles. Toll ½d. Westminster Bridge is a structure of great simplicity, with a sufficient admixture of solidity and grandeur as to give it ...

DOMESTIC ENTERTAINMENT

In the nineteenth century many families would spend their evenings and free time at home reading out loud, writing and putting on plays, performing music, singing songs, playing games and cards, and dancing. The Dickens family, with their considerable musical and literary talents, were no exception, and from an early age Charles and his pianist sister Fanny would entertain the household with their performances. Dickens wrote his first play, *Misnar, the Sultan of India*, aged about nine. It does not survive, but the fact of its composition is evidence of his burgeoning writing ability and interest. He continued to enjoy putting on theatricals at home throughout his life, and it was an important part of his own children's upbringing, particularly from the 1840s onwards. A new kind of home entertainment that was very popular during the nineteenth century was the miniature or toy theatre. A friend of the family made one for Charles Dickens and his siblings when they were children, but it was possible to buy extremely sophisticated versions too, inspired by real theatres, with moving side wings, lamps and even trap doors for the scenery to come up onto the stage. Sheets of varying prices with scenes, characters and props for popular contemporary plays were available to buy. Charles Dickens's son Charley had fond memories of the miniature theatre in their nursery and his father's delight in performing plays in it. *Oliver Twist* was the only novel by Dickens that was adapted for miniature theatre.

THE LETHARGIC YOUTH contrived without any additional rousing, to set out two card-tables; the one for Pope Joan, and the other for whist. The whist-players were, Mr. Pickwick and the old lady; Mr. Miller and the fat gentleman. The round game comprised the rest of the company.

The rubber was conducted with all that gravity of deportment, and sedateness of demeanour, which befit the pursuit entitled 'whist'—a solemn observance, to which, as it appears to us, the title of 'game' has been very irreverently and ignominiously applied. The round-game table on the other hand, was so boisterously merry, as materially to interrupt the contemplations of Mr. Miller, who not being quite so much absorbed as he ought to have been, contrived to commit various high crimes and misdemeanours, which excited the wrath of the fat gentleman to a very great extent, and called forth the good-humour of the old lady in a proportionate degree...

Isabella Wardle and Mr. Trundle 'went partners,' and Emily Wardle and Mr. Snodgrass did the same; and even Mr. Tupman and the spinster aunt, established a joint-stock company of fish and flattery. Old Mr. Wardle was in the very height of his jollity; and he was *so* funny in his management of the board, and the old ladies were *so* sharp after their winnings, that the whole table was in a perpetual roar of merriment and laughter. There was one old lady who always had about half a dozen cards to pay for, at which everybody laughed, regularly every round; and when the old lady looked cross at having to pay, they laughed louder than ever; on which the old lady's face gradually brightened up, till at last she laughed louder than any of them. Then, when the spinster aunt got 'matrimony,' the young ladies laughed afresh, and the spinster aunt seemed disposed to be pettish; till, feeling Mr. Tupman squeezing her hand under the table, *she* brightened up too, and looked rather knowing as if matrimony in reality were not quite as far off as some people thought for; whereupon everybody laughed again, and especially old Mr. Wardle, who enjoyed a joke as much as the youngest.

The Pickwick Papers, **Chapter 6**.

Pack of Cards, *c.* 1800

'"Miller ought to have trumped the diamond, oughtn't he Sir?" said the old lady. Mr Pickwick nodded assent' (*The Pickwick Papers*, Chapter 6)

Oxford, Bodleian Library, JJ Playing Cards

The Ivy Green, c. 1840
Music composed by Henry Russell.

Dickens's poem 'The Ivy Green' makes an appearance as a composition by the clergyman in *The Pickwick Papers*.

Oxford, Bodleian Library, Mus. Voc. I 50 (47), cover and pp. 2–3

'YOU MUST EXCUSE my talking about this old place, Mr. Pickwick,' resumed the host, after a short pause—for I love it dearly, and know no other—the old houses and fields seem like living friends to me: and so does our little church with the ivy,—about which, by-the-by, our excellent friend there, made a song when he first came amongst us. Mr. Snodgrass, have you anything in your glass?'

'Plenty, thank you,' replied that gentleman, whose poetic curiosity had been greatly excited by the last observations of his entertainer. 'I beg your pardon, but you were talking about the song of the Ivy.'

'You must ask our friend opposite about that,' said the host knowingly: indicating the clergyman by a nod of his head.

'May I say that I should like to hear you repeat it, Sir?' said Mr. Snodgrass.

'Why really,' replied the clergyman, 'it's a very slight affair; and the only excuse I have for having ever perpetrated it, is, that I was a young man at the time. Such as it is, however, you shall hear it if you wish.'

A murmur of curiosity was of course the reply; and the old gentleman proceeded to recite, with the aid of sundry promptings from his wife, the lines in question. 'I call them,' said he,

The Ivy Green
Oh, a dainty plant is the Ivy green,
That creepeth O'er ruins old!
Of right choice food are his meals, I ween,
In his cell so lone and cold.
The wall must be crumbled, the stone decayed,
To pleasure his dainty whim:
And the mouldering dust that years have made,
Is a merry meal for him.
Creeping where no life is seen,
A rare old plant is the Ivy green....

The Pickwick Papers, **Chapter 6.**

Cotillon XVI, *c.* 1785
From *Sixteen cotillons, sixteen minuets, twelve allemands and twelve hornpipes*, composed by J. Fishar.

In *The Mystery of Edwin Drood* Mr Grewgious complains: 'I feel, on these premises, as if I was a bear—with the cramp—in a youthful Cotillon' (Chapter 9). The Cotillon was a dance that originated in France. Literally meaning 'petticoat', the name refers to the flash of the women's undergarments as they changed partners in the dance.

Oxford, Bodleian Library, Harding Mus. F 364, p. 19

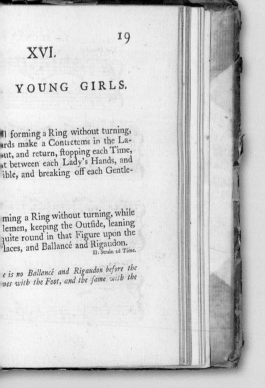

THE LIGHT CAME SPARKLING in among the scarlet runners, as if the churchyard winked at Mr. Mould, and said, 'We understand each other,' and from the distant shop a pleasant sound arose of coffin-making and a low melodious hammer, rat, tat, tat, tat, alike promoting slumber and digestion.

'Quite the buzz of insects,' said Mr. Mould, closing his eyes in a perfect luxury. 'It puts one in mind of the sound of animated nature in the agricultural districts. It's exactly like the woodpecker tapping.'

'The woodpecker tapping the hollow *elm* tree,' observed Mrs. Mould, adapting the words of the popular melody to the description of wood commonly used in the trade.

'Ha ha!' laughed Mr. Mould. 'Not at all bad, my dear. We shall be glad to hear from you again, Mrs. M. Hollow elm tree, eh? Ha ha! Very good indeed. I've seen worse than that in the Sunday papers, my love.'

Martin Chuzzlewit, **Chapter 25.**

The Wood pecker, A Ballad, c. 1815

Written by Thomas Moore; composed by Michael Kelly.

The 'Woodpecker tapping' song is mentioned in both *Martin Chuzzlewit* (see previous page) and *Bleak House*: "'Ah!' said Mr. Bucket. "Here we are, and a nice retired place it is. Puts a man in mind of the country house in the Woodpecker-tapping, that was known by the smoke which so gracefully curled'" (Chapter 57).

Oxford, Bodleian Library, Harding Mus. G. 254 (7), cover and p. 201

The Village Coquettes, 1836

Dickens wrote the libretto to this comic opera in two acts. His sister Fanny, the pianist, introduced him to the composer John Pyke Hullah, who wrote the music.

36.496, title page

THE SIZE of my theatre fascinated my father, and, in conjunction with Clarkson Stanfield, who had been distinguished as a scene painter before he became a member of the Royal Academy, he set to work to produce the first piece. This, I remember was a spectacle called the 'Elephant of Siam,' and its production on a proper scale of splendor necessitated the designing and painting of several new scenes, which resulted in such a competition between my father and Stanfield that you would have thought their very existences depended on the mounting of this same elephant. And even after Stanfield had had enough of it my father was still hard at work, and pegged away at the landscapes and architecture of Siam with an amount of energy which in any man would have been extraordinary, but which I soon learned to look upon as quite natural in him. This particular form of dramatic fever wore itself out after the piece was produced, I remember, and the theatre—much to my delight, for I had hitherto had but little to do with it—found its way to the nursery, where in process of time a too realistic performance of the miller and his men, comprising an injudicious expenditure of gunpowder and red-fire, brought about the catastrophe which finishes the career of most theatres, and very nearly set fire to the house as well.

Charles Culliford Dickens, 'Glimpses of Charles Dickens', *North American Review*, vol. 160, no. 462, May 1895.

A nineteenth-century English miniature theatre

Image © Peter Baldwin/Benjamin Pollock's Toyshop

Oliver Twist miniature theatre sheets, *c.* 1875

Oliver Twist was the only one of Dickens's novels that was adapted for miniature theatre. Sheets could be bought with illustrations to be cut out, mounted on a wire 'slide' and moved in and out of a scene. A range of scenery and backdrops relating to the novel were also available.

Oxford, Bodleian Library, Miniature Theatre 3 (5a), Miniature Theatre 3 (22b), Miniature Theatre 4 (22b) and (26b)

PERFORMING DICKENS

Dickens's love of performing began at an early age at home. Before long, his father was taking the young Charles and his older sister Fanny to the Mitre Tavern in Chatham where they would perform comic songs. Such experiences in front of a proper audience were instrumental in fostering the young Charles's taste for performing and applause that remained all his life. His love of comic songs and playing the fool is well documented. He performed, wrote, sang and stage-managed plays at his parents' house and performed magic shows for his own son Charley's birthdays. However, this love of performance went beyond the domestic: Dickens was a passionate theatregoer who learnt his heroes' parts off by heart. In 1832 he almost became a professional actor but missed the audition because of illness. He remained closely involved with the stage and regularly put on plays with friends both privately and in public theatres. In 1845 he and John Forster organised performances of Ben Jonson's *Every Man in his Humour* and this was followed by several other productions in the following decades. Dickens's two passions, acting and writing, were finally united when he began to give readings of his work. Initially he just read to small groups of friends: a reading of *The Chimes* was the first in 1844. By December 1853 he was reading publicly to audiences of 6,000 for free. It was not long before he was persuaded to take advantage of the fortune that was waiting to be made. In 1858 Dickens gave his first paid reading and began a new, supremely successful, chapter in his professional life. Readings took up much of his time for the next few years; he performed all over England, Ireland and Scotland, and in the winter of 1867/8 embarked upon a triumphant tour of America. His readings, particularly those in the USA, made him a fortune.

I MAY SAY NOW that if ever a man seemed to have been born for one particular pursuit it was my father in connection with the stage. He was, indeed, a born actor and no line of character that I ever saw him essay came amiss to him. From Captain Bobadil to Justice Shallow, from old-fashioned farce such as *Two o'clock in the Morning* and *Animal Magnetism*, to the liveliest Charles Mathewsisms, and thence again to the intensest Frederic Lemaitre melodrama, from the tremendous power of the Sikes and Nancy Reading to the absurdities of Serjeant Buzfuz, from the pathos of Little Dombey to the broad humours of Mrs. Gamp, everything seemed to come natural to him.

Charles Culliford Dickens, 'Glimpses of Charles Dickens', *North American Review,* vol. 160, no. 462, May 1895.

Not So Bad as We Seem playbill, 1851, and Every Man in His Humour playbill, 1850

Playbills for productions in which Charles Dickens performed. The cast lists show, among others, Charles Dickens; his best friend and biographer John Forster; the novelist Wilkie Collins; and the artists Augustus Egg and Frank Stone.

Oxford, Bodleian Library, JJ Dickens Playbills

HANOVER SQUARE ROOMS.

ON TUESDAY EVENING, JUNE 3rd, 1851,
THE AMATEUR COMPANY
OF THE
GUILD OF LITERATURE & ART;

To encourage Life Assurance and other Provident habits among Authors and Artists ; to render such assistance to both as shall never compromise their independence ; and to found a new Institution where honorable rest from arduous labour shall still be associated with the discharge of congenial duties;

WILL HAVE THE HONOR OF PERFORMING, FOR THE THIRD TIME,
A NEW COMEDY, IN FIVE ACTS, BY SIR EDWARD BULWER LYTTON, BART.,
CALLED

NOT SO BAD AS WE SEEM:
OR,
MANY SIDES TO A CHARACTER.

THE DUKE OF MIDDLESEX,	Peers attached to the Son of James II., commonly called the First Pretender	Mr. FRANK STONE.
THE EARL OF LOFTUS,		Mr. DUDLEY COSTELLO.
LORD WILMOT,	A Young Man at the head of the Mode more than a Century old, Son to LORD LOFTUS	Mr. CHARLES DICKENS.
Mr. SHADOWLY SOFTHEAD,	A Young Gentleman from the City, Friend and Double to LORD WILMOT	Mr. DOUGLAS JERROLD.
Mr. HARDMAN,	A Rising Member of Parliament, and Adherent to Sir Robert Walpole	Mr. JOHN FORSTER.
SIR GEOFFREY THORNSIDE,	A Gentleman of good Family and Estate	Mr. MARK LEMON.
Mr. GOODENOUGH EASY,	in Business, Highly Respectable, and a Friend of Sir Geoffrey	Mr. F. W. TOPHAM.
LORD LE TRIMMER,	-	Mr. PETER CUNNINGHAM.
SIR THOMAS TIMID,	-	Mr. WESTLAND MARSTON.
COLONEL FLINT,	-	Mr. R. H. HORNE.
Mr. JACOB TONSON,	(A Bookseller)	Mr. CHARLES KNIGHT.
SMART,	(Valet to LORD WILMOT)	Mr. WILKIE COLLINS.
HODGE, (Servant to SIR GEOFFREY THORNSIDE)		Mr. JOHN TENNIEL.
PADDY O'SULLIVAN,	(Mr. FALLEN'S Landlord)	Mr. ROBERT BELL.
Mr. DAVID FALLEN,	(Grub Street Author and Pamphleteer)	Mr. AUGUSTUS EGG.
LORD STRONGBOW, SIR JOHN BRUIN, Coffee-House Loungers,		Drawers, Watchmen, Newsman.
LUCY, (Daughter to SIR GEOFFREY THORNSIDE)		Mrs. HENRY COMPTON.
BARBARA, (Daughter to Mr. EASY)		Miss ELLEN CHAPLIN.
THE SILENT LADY OF DEADMAN'S LANE,	-	Mrs. COE.

SCENERY.

Lord Wilmot's Lodgings,		Painted by	Mr. PITT.
"The Murillo"		"	Mr. ABSOLON.
Sir Geoffrey Thornside's Library,		"	Mr. PITT.
Will's Coffee House,		"	Mr. PITT.
The Streets, and Deadman's Lane,		"	Mr. THOMAS GRIEVE.
The distrest Poet's Garret, (after Hogarth)		"	Mr. PITT.
The Mall in the Park,		"	Mr. TELBIN.
An open space near the River,		"	Mr. STANFIELD, R.A.
Tapestry Chamber in Deadman's Lane,		"	Mr. LOUIS HAGHE.
The Act Drop,		"	Mr. ROBERTS, R.A.

The performance to conclude with (for the second time) an Original Farce, in One Act, by Mr. CHARLES DICKENS and Mr. MARK LEMON, entitled

MR. NIGHTINGALE'S DIARY.

Mr. NIGHTINGALE,	-	Mr. DUDLEY COSTELLO.
Mr. GABBLEWIG,	(of the Middle Temple)	Mr. CHARLES DICKENS.
TIP,	(his Tiger)	Mr. AUGUSTUS EGG.
SLAP,	(professionally Mr. Flormiville)	Mr. MARK LEMON.
LITHERS,	(Landlord of the "Water Lily")	Mr. WILKIE COLLINS.
ROSINA,	-	Miss ELLEN CHAPLIN.
SUSAN,	-	Mrs. COE.

The Proscenium by Mr. CRACE. The Theatre constructed by Mr. SLOMAN, Machinist of the Royal Lyceum Theatre. The Properties and Appointments by Mr. G. FOSTER. The Costumes (with the exception of the Ladies' Dresses, and the Dresses of the Farce, which are by Messrs. NATHAN, of Titchbourne Street) made by Mr. BARNETT, of the Theatre Royal, Haymarket.
UNDER THE SUPERINTENDENCE OF MR. AUGUSTUS EGG, A.R.A.
Ferruquier, Mr. WILSON, of the Strand. Prompter, Mr. COE.

THE WHOLE PRODUCED UNDER THE DIRECTION OF MR. CHARLES DICKENS.

THE BAND WILL BE UNDER THE DIRECTION OF MR. LAND.

TICKETS (all the Seats being reserved), 10s. each,
To be had of Mr. MITCHELL, 33, Old Bond Street; Messrs. EBERS, 27, Old Bond Street; Mr. HOOKHAM, 15, Old Bond Street; Mr. ANDREWS, 167, New Bond Street; Messrs. CHAPPELL, 50, New Bond Street; Mr. ROBERT OLLIVIER, 19, Old Bond Street; Mr. SAMS, 1, St. James's Street; Messrs. CRAMER and BEALE, 201, Regent Street; Messrs. SMITH and ELDER, 65, Cornhill; and Messrs. KEITH and PROWSE, 48, Cheapside.

DOORS OPEN AT A QUARTER BEFORE SEVEN;
TO COMMENCE AT EXACTLY A QUARTER BEFORE EIGHT O'CLOCK.
THE WHOLE OF THE AUDIENCE ARE PARTICULARLY RECOMMENDED TO BE SEATED BEFORE A QUARTER TO EIGHT.

KNEBWORTH.

ON WEDNESDAY, NOVEMBER 20th, 1850.
WILL BE PERFORMED
BEN JONSON'S COMEDY
OF

EVERY MAN
IN
HIS HUMOUR.

Costumiers, Messrs. NATHAN, of Titchbourne Street.   Perruquier, Mr. WILSON, of the Strand.

Knowell,	(an Old Gentleman)	Mr. DELMÉ RADCLIFFE.
Edward Knowell,	(his Son)	Mr. HENRY HAWKINS.
Brainworm,	(the Father's Man)	Mr. MARK LEMON.
George Downright,	(a Plain Squire)	Mr. FRANK STONE.
Wellbred,	(his Half-brother)	Mr. HENRY HALE.
Kitely,	(a Merchant)	Mr. JOHN FORSTER.
Captain Bobadil,	(a Paul's Man)	Mr. CHARLES DICKENS.
Master Stephen,	(a Country Gull)	Mr. DOUGLAS JERROLD.
Master Matthew,	(the Town Gull)	Mr. JOHN LEECH.
Thomas Cash,	(Kitely's Cashier)	Mr. FREDERICK DICKENS.
Oliver Cobb,	(a Water-bearer)	Mr. AUGUSTUS EGG.
Justice Clement,	(an old merry Magistrate)	The HON. ELIOT YORKE.
Roger Formal,	(his Clerk)	Mr. PHANTOM.
Dame Kitely,	(Kitely's Wife)	Miss ANNE ROMER.
Mistress Bridget,	(his Sister)	Miss HOGARTH.
Tib,	(Cob's Wife)	Mr. MARK LEMON.

(Who has most kindly consented to act, in lieu of MRS. CHARLES DICKENS, disabled by an accident.)

THE EPILOGUE BY MR. DELMÉ RADCLIFFE.

To conclude with MR. POOLE'S Farce of

TURNING THE TABLES.

Details from playbills for *Nicholas Nickleby*, 1839; *Little Nelly*, 1871; *Martin Chuzzlewit*, c. 1844; and *Dombey and Son*, 1848

Dickens's novels were constantly being adapted for the stage—sometimes even before the book was finished. Dickens himself was never directly involved in their adaptation or production—in the early days they were done without his permission or approval and were blatantly cashing in on his success. The plays were extremely popular and as time went on Dickens gave his blessing to many of them.

Oxford, Bodleian Library, JJ Dickens Playbills

FOR A BOSTON AUDIENCE, his reception is remarkably enthusiastic. Seldom does the polished ice of this proper community crack as loudly, and as cheerily … as it did to-night when Dickens stood before them, and while cheer after cheer broke forth, and cries of welcome and clapping … rose … in a friendly roar, tried to speak and was defeated, and returned gallantly to the charge again, but had scarcely got as far as 'Ladies,' when he was obliged to succumb, and made another dash at 'Gentlemen,' and gave it up, and at last saw that one Englishman was nothing to so many hundred Yankees, and waited smiling and bowing until they had their will, and were ready to let him have his.

The very first words 'Marley was dead, to begin with! That was certain,'—settled the question of success. The way in which those words were uttered, showed also that the reading was to depend for all effect upon the worth of what was read, and upon the sincerity of the reader. From the first to last there is no trickery in it,—full of action, abounding in gesture, with a voice for every character in every mood: with a face for every man, woman, and child, reflecting every feeling. There is no straining for stage effect, no attitudizing, no affectation. The most effective reading we ever listened to—it was the most beautifully simple, straightforward, hearty piece of painting from life. Dear *Bob Cratchit* made twenty-five hundred friends before he had spoken two words, and if everybody had obeyed the impulse of his heart, and sent him a Christmas goose, he would have been suffocated in a twinkling, under a mountain of poultry. As for the delightful *Fizziwigs* [sic] … [p]robably never was a ball so thoroughly enjoyed as the one given by these worthy people to their apprentices. The greatest hit of the evening was the point where the dance executed by *Mr. and Mrs. Fizziwigs* to *Miss Fizziwigs* was described. The contagion of the audiences laughter reached Mr Dickens himself, who with difficulty brought out the inimitable drollery: 'after which Mr. Fizziwig cut positively—cut so that a light seemed to shine from his very calves—and he actually WINKED with his legs.' This was too much for Boston and I thought the roof would go off.

New-York Tribune, **3 December 1867 (front page)**

The Story of Little Dombey, 1858
This was the version specially prepared by Dickens himself for his readings. It was published in the hope it would sell well—but it didn't.

Oxford, Bodleian Library, Dunston B 698

Dickens's own honest if not modest assessment of how the American tour was going:

I CANNOT CONVEY TO YOU an adequate idea of last night's tremendous success. The City is absolutely mad about it. The reception was magnificent, and the 'go' of the Reading without any approach to a precedent in these parts. Nothing that we could have imagined or hoped for, could have surpassed the reality.

Extract from a letter from Charles Dickens to W.H. Wills, 3 December 1867

Portrait from the *Illustrated London News*, 1870

Dickens retires from his exhausting fifteen year schedule of readings. In spite of this he said, as reported in the *Illustrated London News*, 'I close this episode of my life with feelings of very considerable pain.' A major reason for ending the readings was because he intended 'Henceforth to devote myself exclusively to the art that first brought us together.' In other words, to work on *The Mystery of Edwin Drood*.

Oxford, Bodleian Library, JJ Dickens 12 (17b)

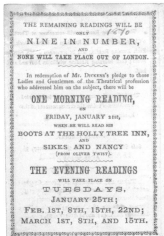

THE REMAINING READINGS WILL BE ONLY 1870

NINE IN NUMBER,

AND

NONE WILL TAKE PLACE OUT OF LONDON.

In redemption of Mr. Dickens's pledge to those Ladies and Gentlemen of the Theatrical profession who addressed him on the subject, there will be

ONE MORNING READING,

ON

FRIDAY, JANUARY 21st,

WHEN HE WILL READ HIS

BOOTS AT THE HOLLY TREE INN,

AND

SIKES AND NANCY

(FROM OLIVER TWIST).

THE EVENING READINGS

WILL TAKE PLACE ON

TUESDAYS,

JANUARY 25TH;

FEB. 1ST, 8TH, 15TH, 22ND;

MARCH 1ST, 8TH, AND 15TH.

The Morning Reading will commence at Three o'Clock, and the Evening Readings at Eight o'Clock. Each Evening Reading will be comprised within two hours; each Morning Reading within an hour and a half.

The Audience is earnestly requested to be seated Ten Minutes before the commencement of the Readings.

PRICES OF ADMISSION.

Sofa Stalls, 7/.   Stalls, 5/.   Balcony, 3/.

Admission, 1/.

Tickets may be obtained at Messrs. CHAPPELL and Co.'s, 50, New Bond Street; MITCHELL'S, 33, Old Bond Street; OLLIVIER'S, 19, Old Bond Street; KEITH, PROWSE, and Co.'s, 48, Cheapside; HAYS'S, 4, Royal Exchange Buildings; and at AUSTIN'S, 28, Piccadilly.

MR. CHARLES DICKENS'S

FINAL

READINGS.

MESSRS. CHAPPELL AND CO.

Have great pleasure in announcing that Mr. CHARLES DICKENS, having some time since become perfectly restored to health,

HAS RESUMED

HIS INTERRUPTED SERIES OF

FAREWELL READINGS,

AT THE

ST. JAMES'S HALL,

LONDON.

Advertisement for 'farewell readings' by Dickens, 1870

This was his final reading tour. He died in June 1870.

Oxford, Bodleian Library, JJ Dickens 12 (19) and (20)

CRIME AND PUNISHMENT

It is hard to believe now that in nineteenth-century London people were still being hanged for a variety of offences, and that their deaths were a public spectacle considered by many an entertaining day out. Taking pleasure in watching someone die in a brutal and violent manner was a long-established tradition stretching back to the amphitheatres of Ancient Rome and beyond, but it was soon to come to an end—and largely due to the efforts of campaigners like Dickens. Newgate, as the prison where felons condemned to death were housed in the nineteenth century, was the appropriate destination for the gallows when they were moved to its vicinity in 1783; when in 1868 hangings ceased to be in public, the gallows were moved inside the gaol's mighty walls. Charles Dickens was horrified by the idea of public executions, as much for the lack of dignity of the condemned as for the 'wickedness and levity' and the 'screeching, and laughing, and yelling in strong chorus' of the crowd. As he writes in his letter to *The Times*, 'I stand astounded and appalled by the wickedness it [public execution] exhibits.' Dickens explored the issue further in his fiction with his portrayal of Dennis the hangman, and the turning bodies of the hanged rioters in *Barnaby Rudge*, and of course the horrific 'reign of terror' of Madame la Guillotine in *A Tale of Two Cities*, which prompts one of the most famous passages in Dickens, spoken by Sidney Carton as he offers his life to save Charles Darnay, the husband of the woman he loves devotedly but hopelessly: 'It is a far, far better thing that I do, than I have ever done; it is a far, far better rest that I go to than I have ever known.'

SIR,

I was a witness of the execution at Horsemonger-lane this morning…

I believe that a sight so inconceivably awful as the wickedness and levity of the immense crowd collected at that execution … could be imagined by no man, and could be presented in no heathen land under the sun. The horrors of the gibbet and of the crime which brought the wretched murderers to it, faded in my mind before the atrocious bearing, looks and language, of the assembled spectators. When I came upon the scene at midnight, the *shrillness* of the cries and howls that were raised from time to time, denoting that they came from a concourse of boys and girls already assembled in the best places, made my blood run cold. As the night went on, screeching, and laughing, and yelling in strong chorus of parodies on Negro melodies, with substitutions of 'Mrs. Manning' for 'Susannah,' and the like, were added to these. When the day dawned, thieves, low prostitutes, ruffians and vagabonds of every kind, flocked on to the ground, with every variety of offensive and foul behaviour. Fightings, faintings, whistlings, imitations of Punch, brutal jokes, tumultuous demonstrations of indecent delight when swooning women were dragged out of the crowd by the police with their dresses disordered, gave a new zest to the general entertainment. When the sun rose brightly—as it did—it gilded thousands upon thousands of upturned faces, so inexpressibly odious in their brutal mirth or callousness, that a man had cause to feel ashamed of the shape he wore, and to shrink from himself, as fashioned in the image of the Devil. When the two miserable creatures who attracted all this ghastly sight about them were turned quivering into the air, there was no more emotion, no more pity, no more thought that two immortal souls had gone to judgment, no more restraint in any of the previous obscenities, than if the name of Christ had never been heard in this world, and there were no belief among men but that they perished like the beasts.

I have seen, habitually, some of the worst sources of general contamination and corruption in this country, and I think there are not many phases of London life that could surprise me. I am solemnly convinced that nothing that ingenuity could devise … could work such ruin as one public execution, and I stand astounded and appalled by the wickedness it exhibits. …

I am, Sir, your faithful servant,
Charles Dickens.

Letter to the Editor, *The Times*, 14 September 1849

Broadside accounts of the execution of Mr. and Mrs. Manning, 13 November, 1849

Dickens was present at this execution and the events he witnessed prompted him to write in protest to *The Times*. Later he based the character of Mademoiselle Hortense in *Bleak House* on Mrs Manning. It was the first time since 1700 that a husband and wife had been hanged together, and this increased the general salacity of the case and public interest in it.

'I shall be brought from my miserable cell, with my wretched wife, and both of us to mount the fatal platform together—to see the rope placed round each other's neck—to die a violent death, in the sight of thousands—it is almost more than I can bear.'

—Letter from the condemned man to his sister.

Oxford, Bodleian Library, JJ Broadsides: Murder and Executions folder 11 (3); JJ Crime 2 (5)

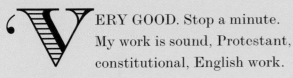

'VERY GOOD. Stop a minute. My work is sound, Protestant, constitutional, English work. Is it, or is it not?'

'No man alive can doubt it.'

'Nor dead neither. Parliament says this here—says Parliament, "If any man, woman, or child, does anything which goes against a certain number of our acts"—how many hanging laws may there be at this present time, Muster Gashford? Fifty?'

'I don't exactly know how many,' replied Gashford, leaning back in his chair and yawning; 'a great number though.'

'Well; say fifty. Parliament says "If any man, woman, or child, does anything again any one of them fifty acts, that man, woman, or child, shall be worked off by Dennis." George the Third steps in when they number very strong at the end of a sessions, and says,

"These are too many for Dennis. I'll have half for *myself* and Dennis shall have half for *him*self;" and sometimes he throws me in one over that I don't expect, as he did three year ago, when I got Mary Jones, a young woman of nineteen who come up to Tyburn with a infant at her breast, and was worked off for taking a piece of cloth off the counter of a shop in Ludgate-hill, and putting it down again when the shopman see her; and who had never done any harm before, and only tried to do that, in consequence of her husband having been pressed three weeks previous, and she being left to beg, with two young children—as was proved upon the trial. Ha ha!—Well! That being the law and the practice of England, is the glory of England, an't it, Muster Gashford?'

Barnaby Rudge, **Chapter 37**

The GROANS Of the Gallows!

OR A SKETCH OF THE

PAST & PRESENT LIFE

OF

WM. CALCRAFT

THE

English Hangman!

COMMONLY CALLED

JACK KETCH.

With a General Review of the causes of Crime, and the Effects of the Punishment of Death.

RIAL, Printer, Monmouth-court, 7 Dials, London.

The Groans of the Gallows! Or a Sketch of the Past & Present Life of Wm. Calcraft the English hangman! commonly called Jack Ketch. With a General Review of the causes of Crime, and the Effects of the Punishment of Death, *c.* 1840

Ned Dennis, the hangman in *Barnaby Rudge*, is thought to be modelled on a real public hangman, Edward Dennis. All executioners were trained at Newgate Gaol during this period.

Oxford, Bodleian Library, JJ Crime 7 (16), front and back cover

Song of the Scaffold.

Hark to the clinking of hammers.
Hark to the driving of nails;
The men are erecting a gallows,
In on of Her Majesty's gaols!
A life—a human life's to be taken,
Which the crowd and the hangman hail;
For the men are erecting a scaffold
In one of Her Majesty's gaols.
'Tis midnight: without its deep silence—
The doom'd wretch in agony moans,
But the clattering still of the hammers
Is drowning the poor victim's groans.
The Chaplain now earnestly prayeth,
To the God of all mercy—for him;
But his mind on his misery strayeth—
For his cup is full to the brim.
Oh pray while you may to your Maker—
His mercy, not justice implore,
Said the priest, while the tears fill'd his eyes,
And his chok'd voice could utter no more;
You ask me to pray, said the felon,
But no one e'er show'd me the way:
'Tis too late, 'tis too late now to teach me.

7 PRISONS AND WORKHOUSES

Of all Charles Dickens's crusades for social justice, his concern with prisons and workhouses was perhaps the most important. He campaigned vigorously through both his novels and his philanthropic work to bring about improvements to the appalling conditions in those institutions. The family's experiences in the Marshalsea debtors' prison when Dickens was young marked him for life. He knew at first hand how it felt to be penniless, cold and desperate, and the memory and fear of these experiences brought realism to his stories and urgency to his philanthropy. Hence the poignancy of Little Dorrit, 'child of the Marshalsea', who has known no other home, caring for her father and spreading goodness in an otherwise hideous and broken world. Prisons loom large in many of Dickens's novels, and his descriptions of them were based on his many visits to gaols and workhouses. He even used the time between his daughter Katey's christening service and the dinner to take two of his guests on a tour around Coldbath Fields Prison (we can only assume that the baby was left behind). In showing innocents like Pip, Oliver, David and Pickwick inside prisons and describing the despair of the workhouse in *Our Mutual Friend*, Dickens was also showing his readers—forcing them to look at the dark underside of life and ask themselves about society's responsibilities to the poor. It is a debate that continues in the twenty-first century: a *Guardian* leader on the concept of 'deserving and undeserving poor', published in the run-up to Dickens's bicentenary in 2012, claimed: 'As we celebrate the 200th anniversary of Charles Dickens, we are witnessing a return of just the sort of language about the poor that he did so much to expose as cruel and inhuman.'

'THIS,' said the gentleman, thrusting his hands into his pockets, and looking carelessly over his shoulder to Mr. Pickwick, 'This here is the hall flight.'

'Oh,' replied Mr. Pickwick, looking down a dark and filthy staircase, which appeared to lead to a range of damp and gloomy stone vaults beneath the ground, 'and those, I suppose, are the little cellars where the prisoners keep their small quantities of coals. Ah! unpleasant places to have to go down to; but very convenient, I dare say.'

'Yes, I shouldn't wonder if they was convenient,' replied the gentleman, 'seeing that a few people live there pretty snug. That's the Fair, that is.'

'My friend,' said Mr. Pickwick, 'you don't really mean to say that human beings live down in those wretched dungeons?'

'Don't I?' replied Mr. Roker, with indignant astonishment; 'why shouldn't I?'

'Live!—live down there!' exclaimed Mr. Pickwick.

'Live down there! yes, and die down there, too, wery often!' replied Mr. Roker; 'and what of that? Who's got to say anything agin it? Live down there!—yes, and a wery good place it is to live in, ain't it?'

The Pickwick Papers, **Chapter 41.**

AT LAST Mr. Micawber's difficulties came to a crisis, and he was arrested early one morning, and carried over to the King's Bench Prison in the Borough. He told me, as he went out of the house, that the God of day had now gone down upon him—and I really thought his heart was broken and mine too. But I heard, afterwards, that he was seen to play a lively game at skittles, before noon.

On the first Sunday after he was taken there, I was to go and see him, and have dinner with him. I was to ask my way to such a place, and just short of that place I should see such another place, and just short of that I should see a yard, which I was to cross, and keep straight on until I saw a turnkey. All this I did; and when at last I did see a turnkey (poor little fellow that I was!), and thought how, when Roderick Random was in a debtors' prison, there was a man there with nothing on him but an old rug, the turnkey swam before my dimmed eyes and my beating heart.

Mr. Micawber was waiting for me within the gate, and we went up to his room (top story but one), and cried very much. He solemnly conjured me, I remember, to take warning by his fate; and to observe that if a man had twenty pounds a-year for his income and spent nineteen pounds nineteen shillings and sixpence, he would be happy, but that if he spent twenty pounds one he would be miserable.

David Copperfield, **Chapter 11.**

The Raquet Ground of the Fleet Prison, 1808 by Augustus Charles Pugin and Thomas Rowlandson, hand coloured print

Mr Pickwick is shown around The Fleet, a debtors' prison, where he is to be imprisoned for failing to pay compensation to Mrs Bardell.

Oxford, Bodleian Library, JJ Crime 9 (29)

King's Bench Prison, 1808 by Augustus Charles Pugin and Thomas Rowlandson, hand coloured print

Along with the Fleet and the Marshalsea, the King's Bench Prison was the third London institution for the incarceration of debtors. David Copperfield visits the bankrupt Mr Micawber during his sojourn at the King's Bench Prison in the Borough.

Oxford, Bodleian Library, J.J Crime 9 (37)

WE WERE AT NEWGATE in a few minutes, and we passed through the lodge where some fetters were hanging up on the bare walls among the prison rules, into the interior of the jail. At that time, jails were much neglected, and the period of exaggerated reaction consequent on all public wrong-doing—and which is always its heaviest and longest punishment—was still far off. So, felons were not lodged and fed better than soldiers (to say nothing of paupers), and seldom set fire to their prisons with the excusable object of improving the flavour of their soup.

Great Expectations, **Chapter 32**.

Newgate Prison, view of the Exterior, 1800 by James Miller

'Those dreadful walls of Newgate, which have hidden so much misery and such unspeakable anguish', writes Dickens in *Oliver Twist* (Chapter 52). There was a prison on the site at Newgate for over 700 years, from 1188 to 1902. The site is now occupied by the Central Criminal Court (the Old Bailey).

Oxford, Bodleian Library, JJ Crime 9 (45)

Newgate Prison, a condemned cell, *c.* 1860s

After his sentencing in *Oliver Twist*, Fagin reflects on the previous inmates of his cell:

'Scores of men must have passed their last hours there. It was like sitting in a vault strewn with dead bodies—the cap, the noose, the pinioned arms, the faces that he knew, even beneath that hideous veil—Light, light!' (Chapter 52).

Oxford, Bodleian Library, JJ Crime 9 (42a)

Gateway at Newgate, with a group of prisoners' friends waiting to be admitted, *c.* 1860s

'From early in the evening until nearly midnight, little groups of two and three presented themselves at the lodge-gate, and inquired, with anxious faces, whether any reprieve had been received.' Mr Brownlow and Oliver at Newgate, in *Oliver Twist* (Chapter 52).

Oxford, Bodleian Library, JJ Crime 9 (42b)

Now, SHE WOULD light upon some poor decent person, like herself, going afoot on a pilgrimage of many weary miles to see some worn-out relative or friend who had been charitably clutched off to a great blank barren Union House, as far from old home as the County Jail (the remoteness of which is always its worst punishment for small rural offenders), and in its dietary, and in its lodging, and in its tending of the sick, a much more penal establishment. Sometimes she would hear a newspaper read out, and would learn how the Registrar General cast up the units that had within the last week died of want and of exposure to the weather: for which that Recording Angel seemed to have a regular fixed place in his sum, as if they were its halfpence. All such things she would hear discussed, as we, my lords and gentlemen and honourable boards, in our unapproachable magnificence never hear them, and from all such things she would fly with the wings of raging Despair.

Our Mutual Friend, **Book 3, Chapter 8**.

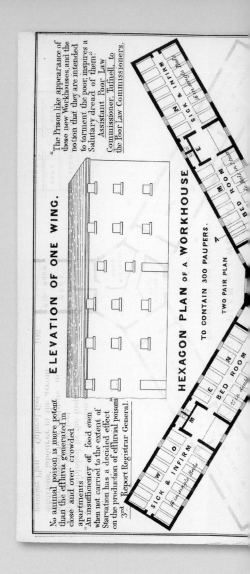

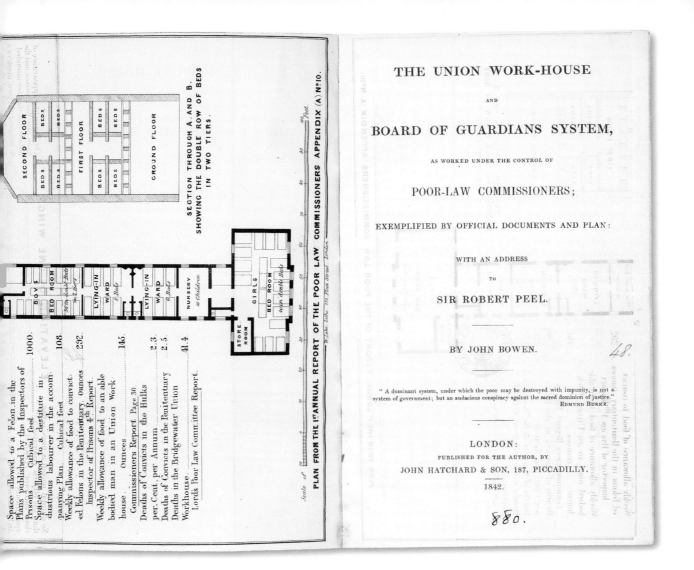

SECOND FLOOR

FIRST FLOOR

GROUND FLOOR

BEDS

SECTION THROUGH A. AND B.
SHOWING THE DOUBLE ROW OF BEDS
IN TWO TIERS.

BOYS
BED ROOM

LYING-IN
WARD

LYING-IN
WARD

NURSERY
10 Children

STORE
ROOM

GIRLS

BED ROOM

PLAN FROM THE 1st ANNUAL REPORT OF THE POOR LAW COMMISSIONERS APPENDIX (A) No. 10.

Space allowed to a Felon in the Plans published by the Inspectors of Prisons .... 1000. Cubical feet.

2do Space allowed to a destitute industrious labourer in the accompanying Plan. 108 Cubical feet.

Weekly allowance of food to convicted Felons in the Penitentiary. 292 ounces. Inspector of Prisons 4th Report.

Weekly allowance of food to an able bodied man in an Union Work house. 145 Ounces. Commissioners Report Page 30

Deaths of Convicts in the Hulks per. Cent. per Annum 2. 3.

Deaths of Convicts in the Penitentiary 2. 5.

Deaths in the Bridgewater Union Workhouse. 41.4 Lords' Poor Law Committee Report.

Scale of

Feet.

W. Lake, litho. 116 Fleet Street, London.

THE UNION WORK-HOUSE

AND

BOARD OF GUARDIANS SYSTEM,

AS WORKED UNDER THE CONTROL OF

POOR-LAW COMMISSIONERS;

EXEMPLIFIED BY OFFICIAL DOCUMENTS AND PLAN:

WITH AN ADDRESS

TO

SIR ROBERT PEEL.

BY JOHN BOWEN.

"A dominant system, under which the poor may be destroyed with impunity, is not a system of government; but an audacious conspiracy against the sacred dominion of justice."
EDMUND BURKE.

LONDON:
PUBLISHED FOR THE AUTHOR, BY
JOHN HATCHARD & SON, 187, PICCADILLY.
1842.

880.

The Union Work-House and Board of Guardians system, 1842

By John Bowen. Plan and title page, showing a hexagon plan of a workhouse, separating sexes, ages and the infirm, with two tiers of beds. Old Betty Higden despairs at the thought of 'a great blank barren Union House' in *Our Mutual Friend*.

Oxford, Bodleian Library, 42.880

UPON THIS, the parish authorities magnanimously and humanely resolved, that Oliver should be 'farmed,' or, in other words, that he should be despatched to a branch-workhouse some three miles off, where twenty or thirty other juvenile offenders against the poor-laws, rolled about the floor all day, without the inconvenience of too much food or too much clothing, under the parental superintendence of an elderly female, who received the culprits at and for the consideration of sevenpence-halfpenny per small head per week. Sevenpence-halfpenny's worth per week is a good round diet for a child; a great deal may be got for sevenpence-halfpenny: quite enough to overload its stomach, and make it uncomfortable. The elderly female was a woman of wisdom and experience; she knew what was good for children; and she had a very accurate perception of what was good for herself. So, she appropriated the greater part of the weekly stipend to her own use, and consigned the rising parochial generation to even a shorter allowance than was originally provided for them…

'What!' said the master at length, in a faint voice.

'Please, sir,' replied Oliver, 'I want some more.'

The master aimed a blow at Oliver's head with the ladle; pinioned him in his arms; and shrieked aloud for the beadle.

The board were sitting in solemn conclave, when Mr. Bumble rushed into the room in great excitement, and addressing the gentleman in the high chair, said,

'Mr. Limbkins, I beg your pardon, sir! Oliver Twist has asked for more!'

There was a general start. Horror was depicted on every countenance.

'For *more*!' said Mr. Limbkins. 'Compose yourself, Bumble, and answer me distinctly. Do I understand that he asked for more, after he had eaten the supper allotted by the dietary?'

'He did, sir,' replied Bumble.

'That boy will be hung,' said the gentleman in the white waistcoat. 'I know that boy will be hung.'

Oliver Twist, **Chapter 2.**

Tables for calculating the quantity of provisions consumed by any number of persons according to the Workhouse Dietary, 1848

These simple multiplication tables show how innumerate the workhouse staff were.

Oxford, Bodleian Library, 1807 e.156(11), centrefold

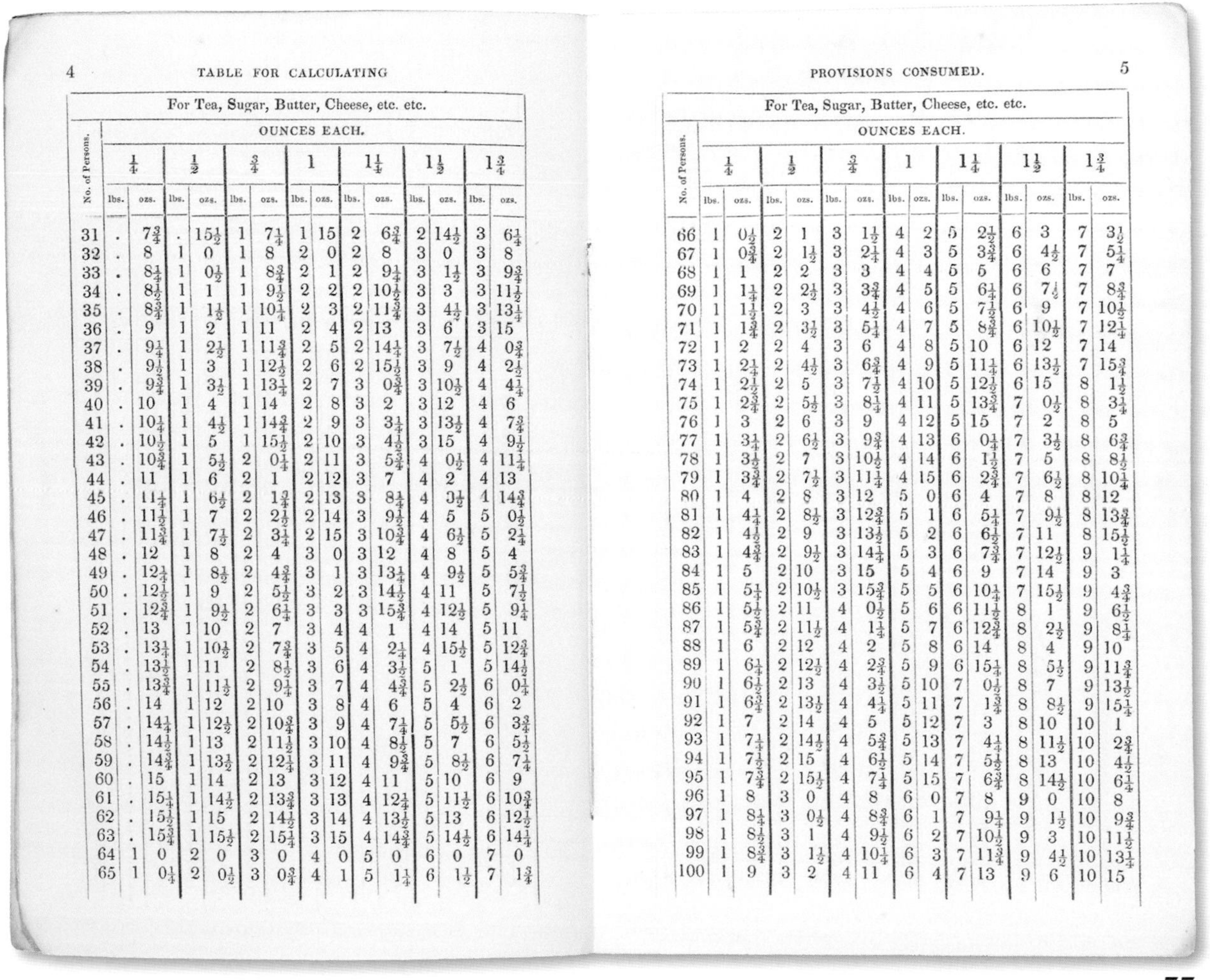

4 TABLE FOR CALCULATING

For Tea, Sugar, Butter, Cheese, etc. etc.

OUNCES EACH.

No. of Persons.	¼		½		¾		1		1¼		1½		1¾	
	lbs.	ozs.	lbs.	ozs.	lbs.	ozs.	lbs.	ozs.	lbs.	ozs.	lbs.	ozs.	lbs.	ozs.
31	.	7¾	.	15½	1	7¼	1	15	2	6¾	2	14½	3	6¼
32	.	8	1	0	1	8	2	0	2	8	3	0	3	8
33	.	8¼	1	0½	1	8¾	2	1	2	9¼	3	1½	3	9¾
34	.	8½	1	1	1	9½	2	2	2	10½	3	3	3	11½
35	.	8¾	1	1½	1	10¼	2	3	2	11¾	3	4½	3	13¼
36	.	9	1	2	1	11	2	4	2	13	3	6	3	15
37	.	9¼	1	2½	1	11¾	2	5	2	14¼	3	7½	4	0¾
38	.	9½	1	3	1	12½	2	6	2	15½	3	9	4	2½
39	.	9¾	1	3½	1	13¼	2	7	3	0¾	3	10½	4	4¼
40	.	10	1	4	1	14	2	8	3	2	3	12	4	6
41	.	10¼	1	4½	1	14¾	2	9	3	3¼	3	13½	4	7¾
42	.	10½	1	5	1	15½	2	10	3	4½	3	15	4	9½
43	.	10¾	1	5½	2	0¼	2	11	3	5¾	4	0½	4	11¼
44	.	11	1	6	2	1	2	12	3	7	4	2	4	13
45	.	11¼	1	6½	2	1¾	2	13	3	8¼	4	0½	4	14¾
46	.	11½	1	7	2	2½	2	14	3	9½	4	5	5	0½
47	.	11¾	1	7½	2	3¼	2	15	3	10¾	4	6½	5	2¼
48	.	12	1	8	2	4	3	0	3	12	4	8	5	4
49	.	12¼	1	8½	2	4¾	3	1	3	13¼	4	9½	5	5¾
50	.	12½	1	9	2	5½	3	2	3	14½	4	11	5	7½
51	.	12¾	1	9½	2	6¼	3	3	3	15¾	4	12½	5	9¼
52	.	13	1	10	2	7	3	4	4	1	4	14	5	11
53	.	13¼	1	10½	2	7¾	3	5	4	2¼	4	15½	5	12¾
54	.	13½	1	11	2	8½	3	6	4	3½	5	1	5	14½
55	.	13¾	1	11½	2	9¼	3	7	4	4¾	5	2½	6	0¼
56	.	14	1	12	2	10	3	8	4	6	5	4	6	2
57	.	14¼	1	12½	2	10¾	3	9	4	7¼	5	5½	6	3¾
58	.	14½	1	13	2	11½	3	10	4	8½	5	7	6	5½
59	.	14¾	1	13½	2	12¼	3	11	4	9¾	5	8½	6	7¼
60	.	15	1	14	2	13	3	12	4	11	5	10	6	9
61	.	15¼	1	14½	2	13¾	3	13	4	12¼	5	11½	6	10¾
62	.	15½	1	15	2	14½	3	14	4	13½	5	13	6	12½
63	.	15¾	1	15½	2	15¼	3	15	4	14¾	5	14½	6	14¼
64	1	0	2	0	3	0	4	0	5	0	6	0	7	0
65	1	0¼	2	0½	3	0¾	4	1	5	1¼	6	1½	7	1¾

PROVISIONS CONSUMED. 5

For Tea, Sugar, Butter, Cheese, etc. etc.

OUNCES EACH.

No. of Persons.	¼		½		¾		1		1¼		1½		1¾	
	lbs.	ozs.	lbs.	ozs.	lbs.	ozs.	lbs.	ozs.	lbs.	ozs.	lbs.	ozs.	lbs.	ozs.
66	1	0½	2	1	3	1½	4	2	5	2½	6	3	7	3½
67	1	0¾	2	1½	3	2¼	4	3	5	3¾	6	4½	7	5¼
68	1	1	2	2	3	3	4	4	5	5	6	6	7	7
69	1	1¼	2	2½	3	3¾	4	5	5	6¼	6	7½	7	8¾
70	1	1½	2	3	3	4½	4	6	5	7½	6	9	7	10½
71	1	1¾	2	3½	3	5¼	4	7	5	8¾	6	10½	7	12¼
72	1	2	2	4	3	6	4	8	5	10	6	12	7	14
73	1	2¼	2	4½	3	6¾	4	9	5	11¼	6	13½	7	15¾
74	1	2½	2	5	3	7½	4	10	5	12½	6	15	8	1½
75	1	2¾	2	5½	3	8¼	4	11	5	13¾	7	0½	8	3¼
76	1	3	2	6	3	9	4	12	5	15	7	2	8	5
77	1	3¼	2	6½	3	9¾	4	13	6	0¼	7	3½	8	6¾
78	1	3½	2	7	3	10½	4	14	6	1½	7	5	8	8½
79	1	3¾	2	7½	3	11¼	4	15	6	2¾	7	6½	8	10¼
80	1	4	2	8	3	12	5	0	6	4	7	8	8	12
81	1	4¼	2	8½	3	12¾	5	1	6	5¼	7	9½	8	13¾
82	1	4½	2	9	3	13½	5	2	6	6½	7	11	8	15½
83	1	4¾	2	9½	3	14¼	5	3	6	7¾	7	12½	9	1¼
84	1	5	2	10	3	15	5	4	6	9	7	14	9	3
85	1	5¼	2	10½	3	15¾	5	5	6	10¼	7	15½	9	4¾
86	1	5½	2	11	4	0½	5	6	6	11½	8	1	9	6½
87	1	5¾	2	11½	4	1¼	5	7	6	12¾	8	2½	9	8¼
88	1	6	2	12	4	2	5	8	6	14	8	4	9	10
89	1	6¼	2	12½	4	2¾	5	9	6	15¼	8	5½	9	11¾
90	1	6½	2	13	4	3½	5	10	7	0½	8	7	9	13½
91	1	6¾	2	13½	4	4¼	5	11	7	1¾	8	8½	9	15¼
92	1	7	2	14	4	5	5	12	7	3	8	10	10	1
93	1	7¼	2	14½	4	5¾	5	13	7	4¼	8	11½	10	2¾
94	1	7½	2	15	4	6½	5	14	7	5½	8	13	10	4½
95	1	7¾	2	15½	4	7¼	5	15	7	6¾	8	14½	10	6¼
96	1	8	3	0	4	8	6	0	7	8	9	0	10	8
97	1	8¼	3	0½	4	8¾	6	1	7	9¼	9	1½	10	9¾
98	1	8½	3	1	4	9½	6	2	7	10½	9	3	10	11½
99	1	8¾	3	1½	4	10¼	6	3	7	11¾	9	4½	10	13¼
100	1	9	3	2	4	11	6	4	7	13	9	6	10	15

THE COMING OF THE RAILWAYS

The coming of the railways was one of the most important developments of the nineteenth century. Travel was revolutionised, as were commerce and communication, becoming dramatically cheaper, faster, more comfortable and reliable. In the early period of railway construction (the 1830s and 1840s) there were many small companies working independently—these were gradually amalgamated as the century progressed. The London & Birmingham railway is the one that features most prominently in Dickens's writing, because it started at Euston Station and then cut right up through North London. The destruction wrought by the construction of the track is difficult to imagine—and neither Dickens nor the engineer who worked on it made much effort to understate its effect. Dickens likened its progress through Camden Town to an earthquake, while the engineer, Peter Lecount, reckoned that building the railway would involve lifting around 700,000,000 cubic metres of material—more than the Great Pyramid of Giza! Disruption continued once the trains were running—they were noisy and dirty—hence the wealthy inhabitants of North London initially insisted that they were pulled on huge ropes and pulleys up the line past their houses, and the coal engines were not lit until they were at Camden Town. Given the lack of safety, it is not surprising that there were several accidents in the first few decades of train travel. Many years later Dickens himself was lucky to survive the Staplehurst Crash in 1865 and in many ways he never got over it. He helped others out of the wreckage and remembered to go back for his unfinished manuscript of *Our Mutual Friend*.

THE FIRST SHOCK of a great earthquake had, just at that period, rent the whole neighbourhood to its centre. Traces of its course were visible on every side. Houses were knocked down; streets broken through and stopped; deep pits and trenches dug in the ground; enormous heaps of earth and clay thrown up; buildings that were undermined and shaking, propped by great beams of wood. Here, a chaos of carts, overthrown and jumbled together, lay topsy-turvy at the bottom of a steep unnatural hill; there, confused treasures of iron soaked and rusted in something that had accidentally become a pond. Everywhere were bridges that led nowhere; thoroughfares that were wholly impassable; Babel towers of chimneys, wanting half their height; temporary wooden houses and enclosures, in the most unlikely situations, carcases of ragged tenements, and fragments of unfinished walls and arches, and piles of scaffolding, and wildernesses of bricks, and giant forms of cranes, and tripods straddling above nothing. There were a hundred thousand shapes and substances of incompleteness, wildly mingled out of their places, upside down, burrowing in the earth, aspiring in the air, mouldering in the water, and unintelligible as any dream. Hot springs and fiery eruptions, the usual attendants upon earthquakes, lent their contributions of confusion to the scene. Boiling water hissed and heaved within dilapidated walls; whence, also, the glare and roar of flames came issuing forth; and mounds of ashes blocked up rights of way, and wholly changed the law and custom of the neighbourhood.

In short, the yet unfinished and unopened Railroad was in progress; and, from the very core of all this dire disorder, trailed smoothly away, upon its mighty course of civilisation and improvement.

Dombey and Son, **Chapter 6.**

The Railway under Construction at Camden Town, 1839

Two wash drawings from *Drawings of the London & Birmingham Railway*, by John C. Bourne.

The building of the railways caused chaos, and many buildings had to be cleared and destroyed in order to make way for it. Dickens lived in this area in the early 1820s and would have remembered it as it was before the railway came. His old school, the Wellington House Academy in Hampstead Road, was much changed when he revisited the area. 'A great trunk-line had swallowed the play-ground, sliced away the schoolroom, and pared off the corner of the house', remembered Dickens in *Household Words*, 1851. Construction of the London & Birmingham line began in November 1833; it was fully opened in September 1838.

Oxford, Bodleian Library, G.A. Eng. rlys a. 1, Plates V and VII

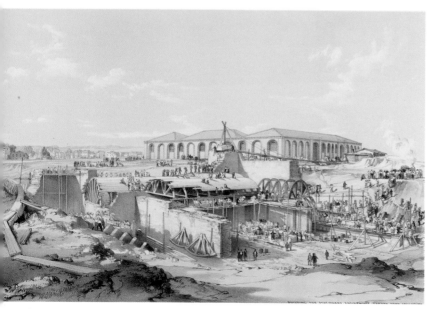

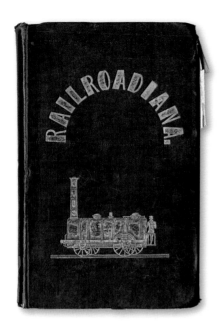

Front cover and map from *Railroadiana, a new history of England, or Picturesque, biographical ... and antiquarian sketches descriptive of the vicinity of the railroads. London and Birmingham railway,* 1838

In *Dombey and Son*, Dickens describes the transformation of Staggs Gardens in North London:

'As to the neighbourhood which had hesitated to acknowledge the railroad in its struggling days, that had grown wise and penitent ... and now boasted of its powerful and prosperous relation. There were railway patterns ... railway journals ... railway plans, maps, views, wrappers, bottles, sandwich-boxes, and timetables; railway hackney-coach and cab-stands; railway omnibuses, railway streets and buildings, railway hangers-on and parasites, and flatterers out of all calculation'.

(Chapter 15).

Oxford, Bodleian Library, GA Eng. rlys 8°1, 1838, front cover and map

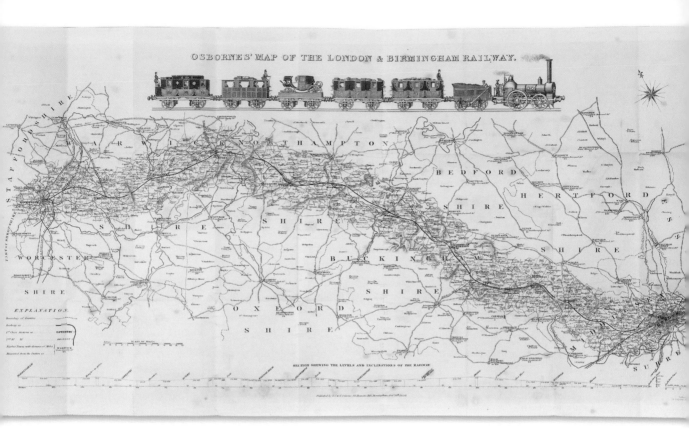

OSBORNES' MAP OF THE LONDON & BIRMINGHAM RAILWAY.

Map from *Osborne's London and Birmingham Railway Guide*, 1840

Mr Dombey travels to Leamington with Major Bagstock on the London & Birmingham railway.

Oxford, Bodleian Library, GA Eng. rlys 16° 98, pp. 4–5

Chalk Farm Bridge (Birmingham Railway), 1840

This charming and possibly slightly idealised image of Chalk Farm Bridge shows the train making its way northwards towards Birmingham. Chalk Farm is just north of Camden Town; it was clearly still part of the countryside surrounding London at this time.

Oxford, Bodleian Library, JJ Railways 24

DREADFUL ACCIDENT ON THE SOUTH-EASTERN RAILWAY, AND LOSS OF TEN LIVES

The two fatal accidents, one at Rednal and the other near Bristol, on the lines of the Great Western Railway company, were followed last week … by one still more disastrous. … The fast tidal train, timed to leave Folkstone at 2.30 p.m. on the arrival of the passengers from Boulogne, who quitted Paris that morning at seven o'clock, started … with about 110 passengers and had proceeded nearly thirty miles … when, at a place called Staplehurst, the accident occurred… It appears that about a mile and a half beyond Headcorn station … there is a bridge, the situation of which is shown in our Engraving, from a sketch made on Saturday morning. … The bridge … which is about 100 ft. in length, and which is supported by six stone piers, crosses a rivulet … which is now nothing more than a muddy ditch. … The fall from the bridge to this ditch is about 15 ft.; the breadth of the ditch itself about 50 ft. Between three and four o'clock in the afternoon several platelayers were employed in laying down new metals on the left-hand side of the bridge on the way to London, and at the end of it nearest Folkestone. Their task was still incomplete, and two lengths, or about 40 ft., of iron rail remained to be laid down on the side of the very track on which the train was advancing. They saw it hasten onward to destruction … and in a few seconds more they saw nine or ten out of the fourteen carriages … precipitated headlong, with their human freight, over the side of the bridge into the ditch beneath. Then ensued such a scene of agony and bewilderment as is … but rarely witnessed. Assistance came … in time to rescue some from positions of the utmost peril, but too late to be of any use to others, whose life had been extinguished in the first terrific crash… At the end of the bridge next to Staplehurst the engine and tender lay partly turned over against a hedge. Immediately behind the tender stood the break [*sic*] van, and a few paces back, suspended as it were from the top of the bridge, with one end buried in the ditch below, was a first-class carriage. At the other end of the bridge stood upon the line the guards' and luggage vans, which

The Staplehurst accident, *Illustrated London News*, 17 June 1865

Dickens was lucky not to have been hurt in this accident, and helped the injured to safety. He had to keep his presence on the train quiet later at the inquest because he was travelling with Ellen Ternan and did not want his relationship with her to cause a scandal.

Oxford, Bodleian Library, 2288 b.6, p. 572

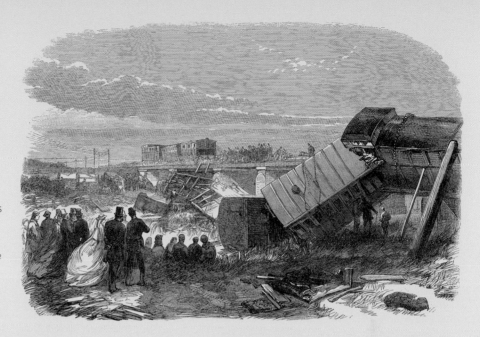

were in the rear of the train, and which were altogether uninjured. A little in front of them were two second-class carriages, with one end resting on the bridge and the other in the ditch... Between these two extremes and all across the ditch, huddled and crashed and forced into one another, lay the five or six first-class carriages which formed the centre of the train. Through their broken sides and shattered windows were to be seen protruding human legs, and arms, and heads, and from every one of them was to be heard the piercing cry

of human suffering... Some who survived, and might have recovered from the injuries inflicted on them by the shock, were smothered in the liquid mud in which they were imbedded... Some, on the other hand, escaped with barely a scratch; but there were few indeed in that heap of ruin who did not bring away with them some token of the tremendous ordeal through which they had passed. ... Mr Charles Dickens was a passenger in the train, but escaped injury.

Illustrated London News, **17 June 1865, pp. 571–2**

 FOOD

In 1851, Charles Dickens's wife Catherine published a book, *What Shall We Have for Dinner? Satisfactorily Answered by Numerous Bills of Fare for from Two to Eighteen Persons*, under the pseudonym Lady Maria Clutterbuck. It is a collection of menus, recipes and meal suggestions that she had gathered over the years, and they show not only the things that the Dickenses liked to eat, but also that they loved to entertain at home. The Dickenses were a very social couple and they had a great number of friends. This book is an indication of the happy times of their marriage, before things began to fall apart. The sense that Catherine felt under pressure to be a perfect hostess in order to keep her husband happy and at home is hinted at in the extract from her book, p90. Dickens's novels are full of descriptions of meals and dishes. In later years, when he had rooms above his office in Wellington Street, he often entertained friends by having food brought there, much as Mr Grewgious entertained Edwin Drood by asking his clerk Bazzard to step over 'to the hotel in Furnival's …. For dinner we'll have a tureen of the hottest and strongest soup available, and we'll have the best made-dish that can be recommended, and we'll have a joint (such as a haunch of mutton), and we'll have a goose, or a turkey, or any little stuffed thing of that sort that may happen to be in the bill of fare' (*The Mystery of Edwin Drood*, Chapter 11). It is surprising to discover how common 'take away' food was at this time, much more so than it is now, in an age when many people did not have kitchens or the means to prepare food. There was a multitude of pie and pudding shops, bakers, chop houses, oyster and eel stalls selling cheap, fast food to the people of the city.

WITHOUT another word spoken on either side, the lodger took from his great trunk a kind of temple, shining as of polished silver, and placed it carefully on the table.

Greatly interested in the proceedings, Mr. Swiveller observed him closely. Into one little chamber of this temple he dropped an egg, into another some coffee, into the third a compact piece of raw steak from a neat tin case, into a fourth he poured some water. Then, with the aid of a phosphorus-box and some matches, he procured a light and applied it to a spirit-lamp which had a place of its own below the temple; then he shut down the lids of all the little chambers, then he opened them; and then, by some wonderful and unseen agency, the steak was done, the egg was boiled, the coffee was accurately prepared, and his breakfast was ready.

The Old Curiosity Shop, **Chapter 35.**

Advertisement for the Patent Peripurist, 1828

This was the kind of stove used by the Single Gentleman in the extract above. The nineteenth century saw great advances in appliances of this kind.

Oxford, Bodleian Library, JJ Gas and Gas Appliances 1 (57)

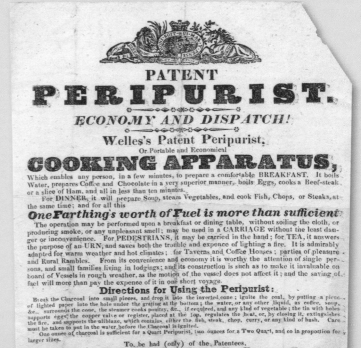

PATENT
PERIPURIST.
ECONOMY AND DISPATCH!
Welles's Patent Peripurist,
Or Portable and Economical
COOKING APPARATUS,
Which enables any person, in a few minutes, to prepare a comfortable BREAKFAST. It boils Water, prepares Coffee and Chocolate in a very superior manner, boils Eggs, cooks a Beef-steak or a slice of Ham, and all in less than ten minutes.

For DINNER, it will prepare Soup, steam Vegetables, and cook Fish, Chops, or Steaks, at the same time; and for all this

One Farthing's worth of Fuel is more than sufficient

The operation may be performed upon a breakfast or dining table, without soiling the cloth, or producing smoke, or any unpleasant smell; may be used in a CARRIAGE without the least danger or inconvenience. For PEDESTRIANS, it may be carried in the hand; for TEA, it answers the purpose of an URN, and saves both the trouble and expence of lighting a fire. It is admirably adapted for warm weather and hot climates; for Taverns and Coffee Houses; parties of pleasure and Rural Rambles. From its convenience and economy it is worthy the attention of single persons, and small families living in lodgings; and its construction is such as to make it invaluable on board of Vessels in rough weather, as the motion of the vessel does not affect it; and the saving of fuel will more than pay the expence of it in one short voyage.

Directions for Using the Peripurist:
Break the Charcoal into small pieces, and drop it into the inverted cone ; ignite the coal, by putting a piece of lighted paper into the hole under the grating at the bottom; the water, or any other liquid, as coffee, soup, &c., surrounds the cone, the steamer cooks poultry, &c., if required, and any kind of vegetable; the tin with holes supports eggs; the copper valve or register, placed at the top, regulates the heat, or, by closing it, extinguishes the fire, and supports the alliblaze, which contains either the fish, steak, chop, curry, or any kind of hash. Care must be taken to put in the water before the Charcoal is ignited.

One ounce of charcoal is sufficient for a Quart Peripurist, two ounces for a Two Quart, and so in proportion for larger sizes.

To be had (only) of the Patentees,
TOZER & Son, 20, Henrietta St. Covent Garden,
at the following Prices, for prompt Payment:—
One Quart 10s. 6d.; Two Quart 20s.; Three Quart 20s.; Four Quart 26s.; Six Quart 29s.;
Eight Quart 31s. 6d. Coffee Pots Extra 2s. 6d and 3s.

ALL BARS ARE snug places, but the Maypole's was the very snuggest, cosiest, and completest bar, that ever the wit of man devised. Such amazing bottles in old oaken pigeon-holes; such gleaming tankards dangling from pegs at about the same inclination as thirsty men would hold them to their lips; such sturdy little Dutch kegs ranged in rows on shelves; so many lemons hanging in separate nets, and forming the fragrant grove already mentioned in this chronicle, suggestive, with goodly loaves of snowy sugar stowed away hard by, of punch, idealised beyond all mortal knowledge; such closets, such presses, such drawers full of pipes, such places for putting things away in hollow window-seats, all crammed to the throat with eatables, drinkables, or savoury condiments; lastly, and to crown all, as typical of the immense resources of the establishment, and its defiances to all visitors to cut and come again, such a stupendous cheese!

Barnaby Rudge, **Chapter 19**.

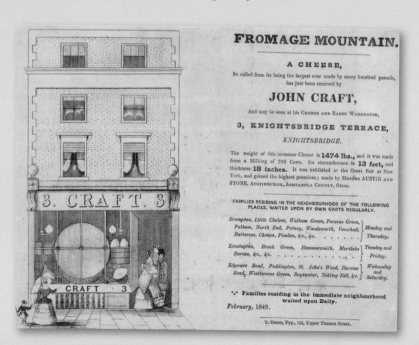

Advertisement, Fromage Mountain, 1849

A cheese similar to that described above is displayed in this shop window. Dickens himself loved cheese and many of the menus in Catherine Dickens's book had a final course at the end of the meal of 'toasted cheese'.

Oxford, Bodleian Library, JJ Food 2 (68)

AND AS IF, in the course of this rubbing and polishing, he had rubbed an enchanted lamp or a magic ring, obedient to which there were twenty thousand supernatural slaves at least, suddenly there appeared a being in a white waistcoat, carrying under his arm a napkin, and attended by another being with an oblong box upon his head, from which a banquet, piping hot, was taken out and set upon the table.

Salmon, lamb, peas, innocent young potatoes, a cool salad, sliced cucumber, a tender duckling, and a tart—all there. They all came at the right time. Where they came from didn't appear; but the oblong box was constantly going and coming, and making its arrival known to the man in the white waistcoat by bumping modestly against the outside of the door; for, after its first appearance, it entered the room no more. He was never surprised, this man; he never seemed to wonder at the extraordinary things he found in the box; but took them out with a face expressive of a steady purpose and impenetrable character, and put them on the table. He was a kind man; gentle in his manners, and much interested in what they ate and drank.

Martin Chuzzlewit, **Chapter 45.**

What Shall We Have for Dinner? Satisfactorily Answered by Numerous Bills of Fare for from Two to Eighteen Persons, by Lady Maria Clutterbuck, 1852

In her introduction to this collection of menus and recipe suggestions based on the food she provided for her husband, family and friends, Catherine (or possibly Charles) Dickens wrote, 'My experience in the confidences of many of my female friends tells me, alas! that … their daily life is embittered by the consciousness that a delicacy forgotten or misapplied; a surplusage of cold mutton or a redundancy of chops; are gradually making the Club more attractive than the Home, and rendering "business in the city" of more frequent occurrence than it used to be in the earlier days of their connubial experience; while the ever-recurring inquiry of "What shall we have for dinner?" makes the matutinal meal a time to dread, only exceeded in its terrors by the more awful hour of dinner!'

Oxford, Bodleian Library, 268 c. 153, title page and pp. 20–21

WHAT SHALL WE HAVE FOR DINNER?

SATISFACTORILY ANSWERED BY NUMEROUS

BILLS OF FARE

FOR FROM TWO TO EIGHTEEN PERSONS.

BY

LADY MARIA CLUTTERBUCK.

A NEW EDITION.

LONDON:
BRADBURY & EVANS, 11, BOUVERIE STREET.
1852.

20   BILLS OF FARE

Salmon. Asparagus Soup. Smelts.
Fore Quarter of Lamb. Fricassee Chickens.
New Potatoes. Peas.
Lobster Patties.
Noyau Jelly. Ice Pudding.
[May to July.]

Asparagus Soup.
Salmon Curry à la Soyer.
Cold Mutton. Minced Collops. Mashed Potatoes.
Salad. Sweet Omelette.
Brocoli au Gratin à la Soyer.
[May to Aug.]

Asparagus Soup.
Turbot. Shrimp Sauce.
Roast Saddle of Mutton. Stewed Pigeons. Mashed and Brown Potatoes. Brocoli. Salad.
Pound Puddings. Macaroni.
[May to Aug.]

Baked Haddock.
Roast Leg of Lamb. Stewed Kidneys. Peas.
Potatoes. Salad.
Cherry Tart. Macaroni.
[May to Aug.]

FOR FOUR OR FIVE PERSONS.   21

Fried Soles. Shrimp Sauce.
Roast Ribs of Lamb. Peas. Potatoes.
Roll Jam Pudding.
[May to Aug.]

Codling. Oyster Sauce.
Beef Steak Pudding, with Kidney and Oysters.
Broiled Fowl. French Beans. Potatoes.
Plum Tart.
Toasted Cheese. Water Cresses.
[May to Aug.]

Salmon. Shrimp Sauce.
Roast Fowl. Boiled Knuckle of Ham. Sheep's Hearts, stuffed. French Beans. Potatoes.
Batter Pudding.
Water Cresses.
[May to Aug.]

Salmon. Shrimp Sauce.
Roast Beef. Cauliflower. Potatoes.
Greengage Tart. Hominy.
Cheese. Water Cresses.
[May to Aug.]

Anchovy toast is included as a savoury in one of the menus in Catherine Dickens's book.

Oxford, Bodleian Library, JJ Food 8 (18)

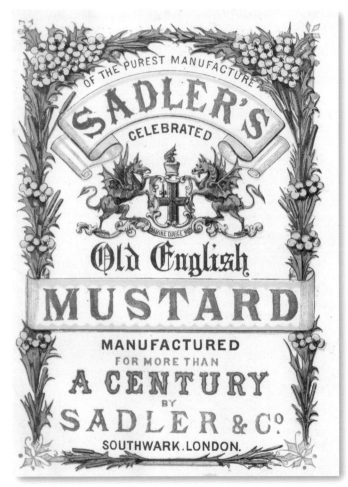

Label for Sadler's Mustard, c. 1868

A beautifully illustrated label from a pot of mustard. It is notable how keen the Victorians were on strong sauces—this was possibly because, in the days before refrigeration, food was not always as fresh as it might have been. Mustard and anchovies would have helped to disguise the taste.

Oxford, Bodleian Library, JJ Food 7 (39a)

Label for Guildhall Sauce, 1860–70

A decorative food label for another sauce that added piquancy to food. It is also an example of the increasingly popular trend of patenting. The illustration represents the Guildhall giants (huge statues known as 'Gog' and 'Magog') which Dickens describes in 'Gone Astray', his account, published in *Household Words*, 1853, of being lost in London at the age of eight or nine. On realising he is lost he plans 'first to go… and see the Giants in Guildhall, out of whom I felt it not improbable that some prosperous adventure would arise…'.

Oxford, Bodleian Library, JJ Food 8 (11)

Goods sold by John Syde, Strand, *c.* 1795

Tradesman's list showing the incredible variety of foods on sale, many of them exotic even today; they were imported from all corners of the globe. David Copperfield describes looking in at the shop windows in this area on his tea-break from working at Murdstone and Grinby's: 'When I had money enough, I used to get half-a-pint of ready-made coffee and a slice of bread-and-butter. When I had none, I used to look at a venison-shop in Fleet Street; or I have strolled, at such a time, as far as Covent Garden Market, and stared at the pine-apples' (Chapter 11).

Oxford, Bodleian Library, JJ Food 1 (22)

Advertisement for Portable Jelly Cakes, 1812

Jelly or Clear Jelly occurs in several of Catherine Dickens's menus as a dessert. The portable jelly cakes would have saved much time in its preparation. Hannah Glasse, in *The Complete Confectioner*, 1800, has a recipe for a Grand Trifle which includes jelly, and she details how to make calves-foot jelly, beginning: 'Take four calves feet, set them on the fire in a saucepan or pot, that will hold two gallons of water and let them boil till they come to pieces', and then you have to set to on dealing with the results! The jelly was a common food for invalids, too: in *The Old Curiosity Shop*, Mr Abel takes delivery of 'a mighty hamper' containing 'fowls ready trussed for boiling, and calves'-foot jelly, and arrow-root, and sago, and other delicate restoratives.' (Chapter 66).

Oxford, Bodleian Library, JJ Food 5 (21)

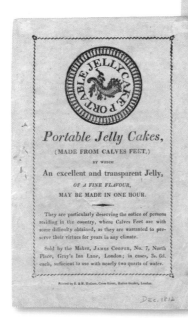

THE NEW ESTABLISHED PATRIOTIC

CHEAP BREAD

Manufactory,

No. 5, NEW STREET,

COVENT GARDEN.

Wᴹ. FOWLER,

BAKER TO HER MAJESTY,

QUEEN CAROLINE,

Most respectfully invites the FRIENDS of REFORM and LOVERS of ECONOMY and RETRENCHMENT, to meet at the above Manufactory, every Day in the ensuing Week, to take into consideration the PRICE of BREAD; and for such a laudable Institution, the Subscriptions are so abundant, that the Establishment is now enabled to sell the very BEST BREAD, at EIGHT PENCE PER LOAF! and it is fully expected, from the very liberal Subscriptions already received, that shortly we shall be enabled to Sell the BEST BREAD, at SIXPENCE PER LOAF!!! and it is hoped that a generous Public will encourage so noble an Institution, by sending to No. 5, NEW STREET, for their Bread and Flour, and *no where else.* This will make the topping Baker come down, and, though reluctantly, say—

> *Of all the shops in Britain blest,*
> *This is the cheapest and the best.*

And the patriotic Baker will reply—

> *And whilst the times remain so hard,*
> *Let others be upon their guard.*

GOD BLESS THE QUEEN!

THE BEST BREAD NOW SELLING AT

No. 5, New Street, Covent Garden,

AT EIGHT PENCE PER LOAF.

Printed by W. GLINDON.   51, RUPERT STREET, Haymarket.

Cheap Bread, *c.* 1810–20

An advertisement for a product that sells itself based on price rather than quality; the forerunner of the mass-produced provender with which we are all too familiar a century and a half later.

Oxford, Bodleian Library, JJ Food 3 (55)

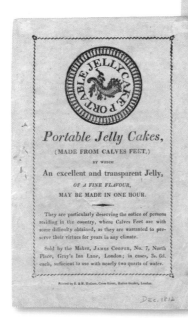

Portable Jelly Cakes,

(MADE FROM CALVES FEET,)

BY WHICH

An excellent and transparent Jelly,

OF A FINE FLAVOUR,

MAY BE MADE IN ONE HOUR.

They are particularly deserving the notice of persons residing in the country, where Calves Feet are with some difficulty obtained, as they are warranted to preserve their virtues for years in any climate.

Sold by the Maker, JAMES COOPER, No. 7, North Place, Gray's Inn Lane, London; in cases, 3s. 6d. each, sufficient to use with nearly two quarts of water.

Printed by E. & H. Hodson, Cross Street, Hatton Garden, London.

Dec. 1812

10 PUBLISHING DICKENS

Charles Dickens was the first writer to popularise the publication of novels in instalments, with the runaway success of *The Pickwick Papers*. His novels were also published in the journals that Dickens edited himself, including *All The Year Round* and *Household Words*. There were many advantages to this method of publication, the greatest being that periodicals were relatively cheap—around a shilling—allowing for a much larger and wider readership. Improvements in literacy in the early nineteenth century meant that there were many more readers—hence the poorer sections of society who could not afford to spend a guinea-and-a-half on a complete novel could now afford to buy and read contemporary literature. This naturally appealed to Dickens the social reformer. The success of *The Pickwick Papers* was such that it provided the template for most of Dickens's novels; this became the rhythm of Dickens's writing life. The instalments or monthly parts typically contained several pages of advertisements, two plates of illustration and around thirty-two pages of text. The novels were all (except *Hard Times* and *Great Expectations*) illustrated and Dickens worked closely with the artists to ensure that the pictures would be as accurate and amusing as possible. He worked with a variety of illustrators, including George Cruikshank, George Cattermole, Marcus Stone and Daniel Maclise, but it was his long collaboration with Hablot Knight Browne—Phiz—that was the most successful.

Bentley's Miscellany, 1837

Oliver Twist first appeared in the periodical *Bentley's Miscellany*, under the pseudonym 'Boz', with illustrations by George Cruikshank.

Oxford, Bodleian Library, Per. 2705 d. 388 (1(1837)) p. 105

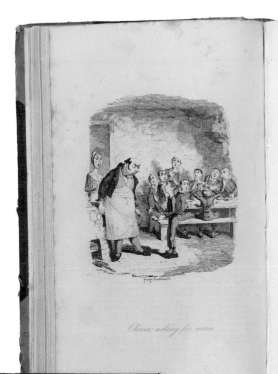

Bound volume of *All the Year Round*, 1860

The previous number (lh page) advertises the first instalment of *Great Expectations*.

Oxford, Bodleian Library, Per. 2705 d. 202 3–4 vol. 4 pp. 168–9

Front wrapper of *The Pickwick Papers*, 1836

The publishers, Chapman & Hall, originally asked Dickens to provide captions for a series of illustrations of 'cockney sporting plates' that they had commissioned. The idea was to exploit the comedy of city folk indulging in country pursuits and getting into scrapes. It was not long before Dickens had got carried away with the story and the text was dictating the pictures—and *Pickwick* was born.

Oxford, Bodleian Library, Arch. AA d. 169/1

Illustration from *The Pickwick Papers* by Phiz, 1836

This illustration shows the introduction of Sam Weller. This character, introduced in the fourth number, immediately struck a popular chord and sales of the serial increased dramatically. Soon there was a whole range of Weller-rated material on sale, including bootleg copies and joke books.

Oxford, Bodleian Library, 250 a. 252, plate facing p. 94

THE LANDLADY FLUNG a pair of lady's shoes into the yard, and bustled away. 'Number 5,' said Sam, as he picked up the shoes, and taking a piece of chalk from his pocket, made a memorandum of their destination on the soles—'Lady's shoes and private sittin' room! I suppose *she* didn't come in the vaggin.'

'She came in early this morning,' cried the girl, who was still leaning over the railing of the gallery, 'with a gentleman in a hackney-coach, and it's him as wants his boots, and you'd better do 'em, that's all about it.'

'Vy didn't you say so before,' said Sam, with great indignation, singling out the boots in question from the heap before him. 'For all I know'd he vas one o' the regular three-pennies. Private room! and a lady too! If he's anything of a gen'lm'n, he's vurth a shillin' a day, let alone the arrands.'

Stimulated by this inspiring reflection, Mr. Samuel brushed away with such hearty goodwill, that in a few minutes the boots and shoes, with a polish which would have struck envy to the soul of the amiable Mr. Warren (for they used Day and Martin at the White Hart) had arrived at the door of number five.

The Pickwick Papers, **Chapter 10**

Even after his harrowing experience at Warren's blacking factory, Dickens could refer to its proprietor as 'amiable', though making Day and Martin's the preferred boot polish of the inn where Sam works.

Illustration from *Oliver Twist* by George Cruikshank, 1838

This illustration shows Fagin in the Condemned Cell in Newgate Prison. Cruikshank also illustrated *Sketches by Boz* and *The Mudfog Papers*.

Oxford, Bodleian Library, 256 e 16981/3, plate facing 295

Illustration from *Our Mutual Friend* by Marcus Stone, 1865

Marcus Stone was the son of Dickens's great friend and illustrator Frank Stone, 'Old Tone'. Dickens took him on as a kind of surrogate son after the death of his father, promoting him professionally and generally looking after him.

Oxford, Bodleian Library, 250 a.261, plate facing p. 211

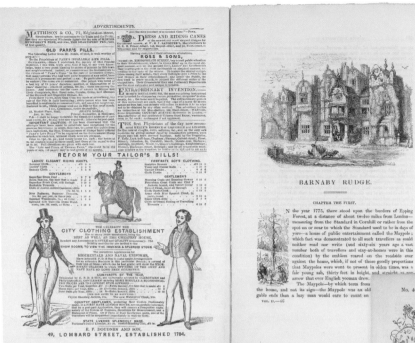

Barnaby Rudge, 1841

Front wrapper and advertisements opposite the first page. Illustration at the beginning of the novel by G. Cattermole.

Dickens launched his weekly periodical *Master Humphrey's Clock* in April 1840. Intended as a miscellany, it was not a success initially and Dickens was forced to begin serialising a novel, *The Old Curiosity Shop*, in order to capture public opinion. The pressure of producing weekly episodes was immense and Dickens became ill. In spite of this, *The Old Curiosity Shop* was one of his most successful novels. *Barnaby Rudge* was the next novel to be serialised.

Oxford, Bodleian Library, Arch. AA d. 88/46

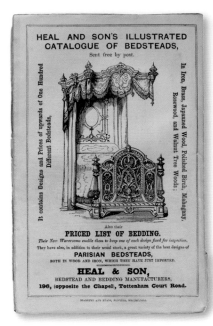

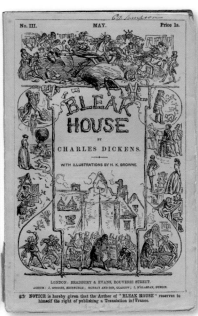

Front and back wrapper of *Bleak House*, May 1852

Illustrations by Phiz. *Bleak House* was the first of three novels by Dickens written in the 1850s that examine the state of the country. Written on a huge scale, it takes as one of its major themes the flaws of the English legal system and the terrible effect it had on people's lives.

Oxford, Bodleian Library, Arch. AA d.40/3

Front wrappers of *Nicholas Nickleby*, February 1839; *Dombey and Son*, May 1847, *Little Dorrit*, March 1857.

Illustrations by Phiz.

Oxford, Bodleian Library, Arch. AA d.59/11; Arch. AA d.105/8; Arch. AA d.155/16

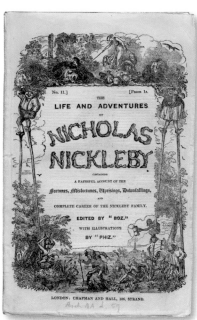

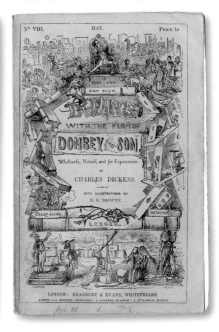

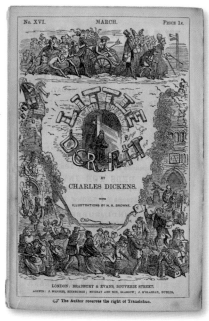

Front wrapper of *The Mystery of Edwin Drood*, April 1870

This was Dickens's last novel and he died before finishing it, leaving the identity of the murderer of Edwin Drood shrouded in mystery. The wrapper has prompted much speculation over what Dickens told Charles Collins about the outcome of the novel. He withdrew because of ill-health soon after designing the wrapper and Luke Fildes illustrated the text. The culprit is generally believed to have been Drood's uncle, John Jasper.

Oxford, Bodleian Library, Arch. AA d. 44/1

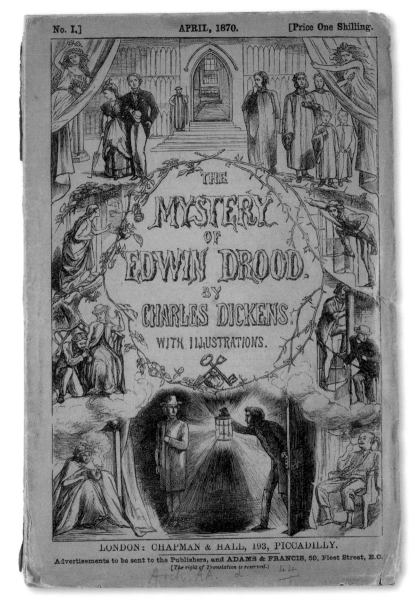

No. I.]   APRIL, 1870.   [Price One Shilling.

THE MYSTERY OF EDWIN DROOD. BY CHARLES DICKENS. WITH ILLUSTRATIONS.

LONDON: CHAPMAN & HALL, 193, PICCADILLY.
Advertisements to be sent to the Publishers, and ADAMS & FRANCIS, 59, Fleet Street, E.C.
[*The right of Translation is reserved.*]

11 THE CHRISTMAS BOOKS

Charles Dickens loved Christmas and celebrated it with great jollity and enthusiasm. In 1843, after a series of devastating experiences that included visiting a Ragged School and reading the Report of the Children's Employment Commission, Dickens decided that something had to be done to prick the consciences of the wealthy out of their complacent indifference towards the appalling plight of the poor. So in October he wrote *A Christmas Carol*. It was published on 19 December in a beautiful, illustrated edition. It sold 6,000 copies before Christmas and continued to sell well into the spring. The following year Dickens continued the *Carol* theme with *The Chimes* and produced five Christmas novellas in total, the others being *The Cricket on the Hearth* (1845), *The Battle of Life* (1846) and *The Haunted Man and the Ghost's Bargain* (1848). All of these Christmas books had a strong, moral, Christian message and were designed to appeal to people's supposed feelings of goodwill during the festive period. *The Chimes* was a popular, critically acclaimed book and sold well, but not as well as its successor, *The Cricket on the Hearth*. By 1845 it seemed that the Victorian public had come to expect a Christmas book and a market had been created. However, the quality of the books was declining and *The Haunted Man* was not so popular—which perhaps explains in part why it was the last in the series. Regardless of how successful these books were, they earned Dickens critical acclaim as a social reformer, went a long way towards creating the image of a Victorian Christmas that we have today, and made a considerable amount of money for the writer and publishers.

'A MERRY CHRISTMAS, uncle! God save you!' cried a cheerful voice. It was the voice of Scrooge's nephew, who came upon him so quickly that this was the first intimation he had of his approach.

'Bah!' said Scrooge, 'Humbug!'

He had so heated himself with rapid walking in the fog and frost, this nephew of Scrooge's, that he was all in a glow; his face was ruddy and handsome; his eyes sparkled, and his breath smoked again.

'Christmas a humbug, uncle!' said Scrooge's nephew. 'You don't mean that I am sure?'

'I do,' said Scrooge. 'Merry Christmas! What right have you to be merry? What reason have you to be merry? You're poor enough.'

'Come then,' returned the nephew gaily. 'What right have you to be dismal? What right have you to be morose? You're rich enough'…

'But I am sure I have always thought of Christmas time, when it has come around—apart from the veneration due to its sacred name and origin, if anything belonging to it can be apart from that—as a good time; a kind, forgiving, charitable, pleasant time; the only time I know of, in the long calendar of the year, when men and women seem by one consent to open their shut-up hearts freely, and to think of people below them as if they really were fellow-passengers to the grave, and not another race of creatures bound on other journeys. And therefore, uncle, though it has never put a scrap of gold or silver in my pocket, I believe that it *has* done me good, and *will* do me good; and I say, God bless it!'

A Christmas Carol, Stave I.

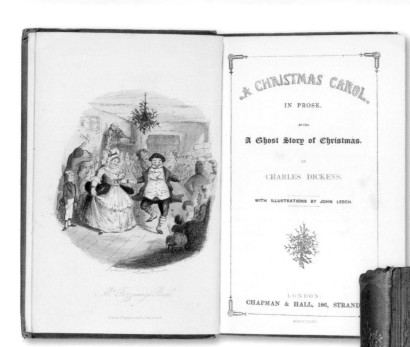

'Mr Fezziwig's Ball', *A Christmas Carol*, **1843**
Illustration by John Leech

'A positive light appeared to issue from Fezziwig's calves. They shone in every part of the dance like moons. You couldn't have predicted, at any given time, what would have become of them next' (Stave II).

Oxford, Bodleian Library, Johnson f.753, frontispiece

A Christmas Carol, **1843**

Oxford, Bodleian Library, Johnson f.753, front cover

The Christmas Books, 1843–48
Red bindings for *The Chimes, The Cricket on the Hearth, The Battle of Life* and *The Haunted Man.*

Dickens insisted that *A Christmas Carol* was beautifully bound in brown cloth and all plates were colour—this significantly reduced the profits made by sales because he also insisted that it only cost 5 shillings. The other Christmas books had no coloured illustrations but were bound in bright red cloth with gilt lettering and edges.

Oxford, Bodleian Library, Vet. A6 f.1236; 256 f.3249; 46.825; Johnson f.755

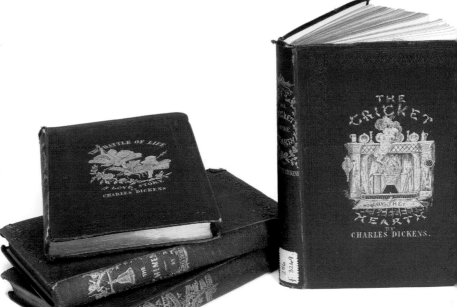

The Chimes: A Goblin Story of Some Bells that Rang an Old Year Out and a New Year In, 1844

Dickens raced back to London from Switzerland to deliver the manuscript of this book and give a reading of it to friends—including the illustrators of both *A Christmas Carol* and *The Chimes*, John Leech and Daniel Maclise.

Oxford, Bodleian Library, Vet. A6 f.1236, frontispiece

105

'A MERRY CHRISTMAS, Bob!' said Scrooge, with an earnestness that could not be mistaken, as he clapped him on the back. 'A merrier Christmas, Bob, my good fellow, than I have given you for many a year! I'll raise your salary, and endeavour to assist your struggling family, and we will discuss your affairs this very afternoon over a Christmas bowl of smoking bishop, Bob! Make up the fires, and buy another coal-scuttle before you dot another i, Bob Cratchit!'

Scrooge was better than his word. He did it all, and infinitely more; and to Tiny Tim, who did NOT die, he was a second father. He became as good a friend, as good a master, and as good a man, as the good old city knew...

He had no further intercourse with Spirits, but lived upon the Total Abstinence Principle, ever afterwards; and it was always said of him, that he knew how to keep Christmas well, if any man alive possessed the knowledge. May that be truly said of us, and all of us! And so, as Tiny Tim observed, God bless Us, Every One!

A Christmas Carol, **Stave V (closing paragraphs)**

Sources and Further Reading

Quotations from Dickens's novels follow the Oxford World's Classics editions published by Oxford University Press.

Quotations from Dickens's letters follow the texts given in *The Letters of Charles Dickens*, Pilgrim Edition, vols 1–12, ed. Madeline House, Graham Storey and Kathleen Tillotsen, Oxford University Press, Oxford, 1965–2002.

Ackroyd, P., Introduction, *Dickens' London: An Imaginative Vision*, Headline Publishing, London, 1987.

Ackroyd, P. *Dickens*, Sinclair-Stevenson, London, 1990.

Baldwin, P., *Toy Theatres of the World*, Rizzoli, New York, 1992.

Bentley, N., M. Slater and N. Burgis, *The Dickens Index*, Oxford University Press, Oxford, 1988.

Callow, S., *Charles Dickens and the Great Theatre of the World*, Harperpress, London, 2012.

Clutterbuck, Lady Maria [Catherine Dickens], *What Shall We Have for Dinner?* London, 1851.

Dickens, C. (ed.), 'Gone Astray', *Household Words*, vol. 7, no. 177, 13 August 1853, p. 553.

Dickens, C. (ed.), 'Our School', *Household Words*, vol. 4, no. 81, 11 October 1851, p. 49.

Dickens, C.C., 'Glimpses of Charles Dickens', *North American Review*, vol. 160, no. 462, May 1895.

Douglas-Fairhurst, R., *Becoming Dickens: The Invention of a Novelist*, Harvard University Press, Belknap Press, Cambridge MA and London, 2011.

Forster, J,. *The Life of Charles Dickens*, Chapman & Hall, London, 1872–74 (3 volumes).

Glasse, H., *The Complete Confectioner*, London, 1800.

Guardian, Editorial, 27 January 2012.

Hawksley, L.D., *Charles Dickens. Dickens' Bicentenary 1812–2012*, Andre Deutsch in association with the Charles Dickens Museum , London 2011.

Illustrated London News, 17 June 1865, pp. 571–2.

Illustrated London News (supplement), 19 March 1870, p. 301.

Mathew, H.G.C., and B. Harrison (eds), *Oxford Dictionary of National Biography: From the Earliest Times to the Year 2000*, Oxford University Press, Oxford, 2004.

New-York Tribune, 3 December 1867.

Pictorial Times, 1846, p. 205.

Schlicke, P., *The Oxford Companion to Charles Dickens*, anniversary edition, Oxford University Press, Oxford, 2011.

Slater, M., *Charles Dickens*, Yale University Press, New Haven; London, 2009.

Tomalin, C., *Charles Dickens: A Life*, Viking, London, 2011.

The Times, Letters to the Editor, 14 September 1849.

Wilson, A.N., *The Victorians*, Hutchinson, London, 2002.

Index

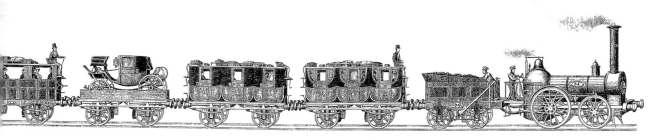

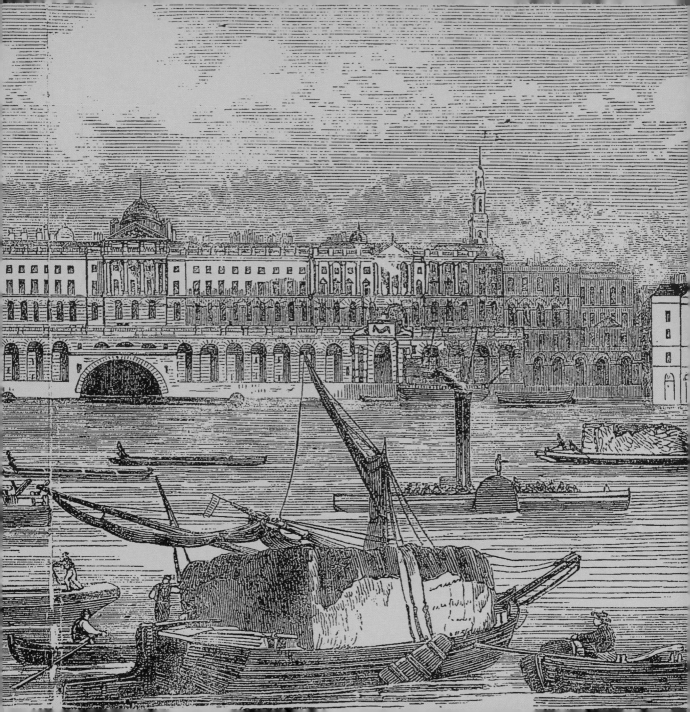